EXCEL 2000

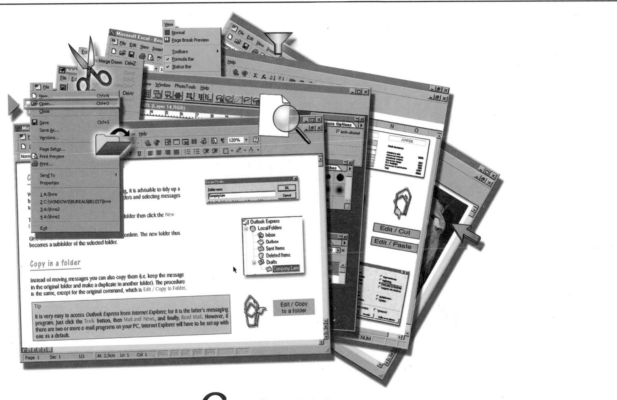

CHOUKA

The author explains the best way to use each command. You gain from a professional's experience of constantly looking for the best way to use the software, i.e. the fastest and simplest. But that's not all! Understanding a command is one thing; understanding how it can be used is another. These two aspects are both covered in the explanations provided.

Often a command can be or must be combined with another command in order to achieve a desired result. There are several types of relationships between commands: combination, complement, extension, etc. Understanding the links between commands is a guarantee of success. In this book, links to other commands are given at the bottom of the page in the form of a string such as: Menu/ Command/Options or Subcommand.

The 'shortcut keys' are combinations of keystrokes that let you execute a command quickly without using your mouse. You are well advised to memorise the shortcuts for the commands you use a lot, because the repetitive movement of the mouse in order to pull down menus and click on commands is tiresome. Not only will you save

quite a bit of time but you will also gain confidence as a user. Whenever a command has a shortcut key, we note it.

Occasionally, a Toolbar button provides another quick way to execute a command. In such cases this is given along with the shortcut key. It's a good compromise between a shortcut key and a menu. It's easier to remember a picture than a string of letters.

A 'paperclip' guide will appear every time the author has something special to say or a tip to give you. It is worth taking note of what this paperclip guide is pointing out to you.

At the end of the book you will find the index. This lists in alphabetical order the important subjects or words and tells you the pages on which these appear in a significant context.

ABOUT THE FULL SCREEN SERIES

The Full Screen series aims to provide a new way of presenting books on software. By flipping quickly through this book, you will already have realised this. You will have gone through a list of menu items identical to those within the program. On the left, the command menu scrolls up and down. All that's missing is the sound of mouse clicks to make you think you're sitting in front of your PC or Mac screen. Since we could not include this characteristic little noise, we have instead highlighted each command.

Except for this detail, your Full Screen book reflects precisely the environment in which you are likely to be working. You are using the very first WYSIWYG (*What You See Is What You Get*) book. With MS Windows used in both home and office settings for some 15 years now, it is high time that the book adapted to most computer users' way of experiencing things.

A new type of book requires a new way of reading. The Full Screen series has been created to meet the specific needs of

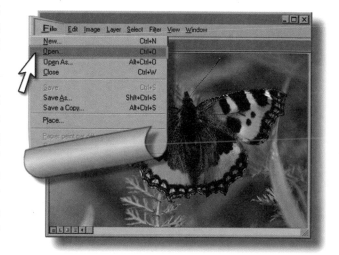

users of various software programs. The book and the program go hand in hand; they move in the same direction. When you encounter a problem, you don't waste time leafing through the book in search of an explanation for a particular command, dialogue box or option. The explanations, suggestions and tips are found in the book in the same places where the command is found in the program. Conversely, you can move just as easily from the book to your screen.

The books in the Full Screen series are intended for beginners. They do not cover all the commands of a software package, because this would make the book unnecessarily complicated (since in some cases there are several hundred such commands!). Through these books you will learn to use the 40 or so commands that lie at the heart of each program – the ones you use on a daily basis in either a professional setting or at home.

Using the menus

A menu contains all the commands on the indicated subject. The File menu, for example, is used to manage files, i.e. open, close, save or print any spreadsheet.

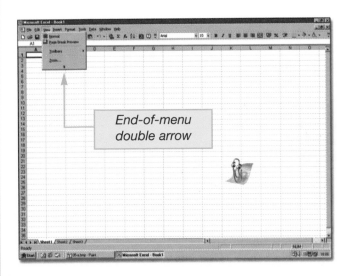

End-of-menu double arrow

To access the commands of a menu you must drop it down. Place the mouse pointer on its name (i.e. point to the menu name) and click the left button.

Some less frequently used commands are hidden by Excel. You can display them by clicking the double arrow that symbolises the end of the menu. The hidden commands are then displayed against a lighter greyed background.

There are three types of commands:

① Commands that open a *dialogue box*, followed by suspension points.
② Commands that have an immediate effect.
③ *Switch-commands,* which, when inactive, look like all other commands but once activated (switched on) are preceded by '✓'.

Some commands are greyed. This means that they cannot be activated because they are irrelevant or inaccessible in the current work context.

Close a menu:

To close a menu just click outside it, or press the *Esc* key.

The Excel 2000 window

The *menu bar* comprises 9 drop-down menus, subdivided into commands. These commands activate the functions we will encounter throughout this book.

The *title bar* indicates the name of the program and the name of the active file (by default: [Book1]).

The *formula bar* is used to create and edit the formulas of the worksheet. It displays the raw contents of the selected cells: characters, if the cell contains characters, or the details of the formula if the cell displays a result.

The *toolbar* contains icons. Each icon acts as a shortcut and carries out the action it symbolises.

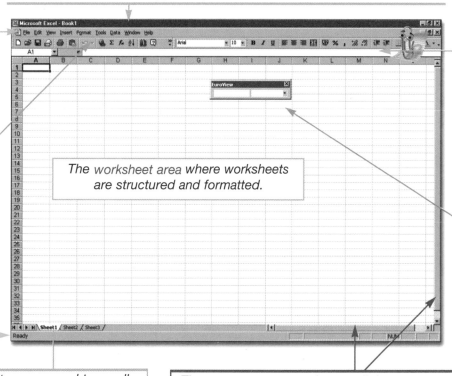

The *worksheet area* where worksheets are structured and formatted.

Floating toolbar. This bar, which is displayed when the program opens, contains the function for Euro conversion.

The *status bar* displays information on the selected command or an operation in progress.

The *tab scrolling buttons* are used to scroll through the spreadsheets of a complex book.

The *scroll bars* are used to scroll the entire spreadsheet vertically and horizontally. Click the scroll bar to scroll in a window, its components or contents.

The formula bar

This bar is used to create new formulas or to edit existing ones. Let us imagine a summary statement of a professional photographer's business expenses.

The cells in the last column show the deductible amount of the expenses from the actual amount disbursed and a variable rate (in %). The result is obtained by simply multiplying the former by the latter.

Click a cell in this last column to select it. The formula bar then displays the references of the selected cell on the left, while on the right is the formula used to calculate the deductible amount. You can of course edit this formula. Note that the selected cell displays only the result in the spreadsheet.

D5	▼	=	=B5*C5	
	A	B	C	D
1		Amount	Deduction	Expenses
2	Food	£2,159.40	100%	£2,159.40
3	Butcher	£993.90	54%	£536.70
4	Baker	£198.30	100%	£198.30
5	Entertainment	£28.20	100%	£28.20
6	Grocer	£178.50	100%	£178.50
7	Restaurant	£381.00	100%	£381.00
8	Caterer	£92.40	54%	£92.40
9	Snack bar	£304.50	100%	£304.50

The references of the selected cell are indicated by a letter (for the corresponding column) and a number (for the row)

MMULT	▼	X ✓ =	=B5*C5	
	A	B	C	D
1		Amount	Deduction	Expenses
2	Food	£2,159.40	100%	£2,159.40
3	Butcher	£993.90	54%	£536.70
4	Baker	£198.30	100%	£198.30
5	Entertainment	£28.20	100%	=B5*C5
6	Grocer	£178.50	100%	£178.50
7	Restaurant	£381.00	100%	£381.00
8	Caterer	£92.40	54%	£92.40
9	Snack bar	£304.50	100%	£304.50

To edit the formula, double click in the cell. In the spreadsheet, the selected cell no longer shows the result, but displays the formula using a colour code. Cells pertaining to the formula are framed in their colour of reference. Edit the formula and click the '✓' in the formula bar to confirm, or the red cross to cancel the change.

Sheet1 / Sheet2 / Sheet3

6
7

Filling a cell

Cells accept various types of content. Figures and formulas are of course most common, but you can fill a cell with up to 32,000 characters of text (some ten A4 pages).

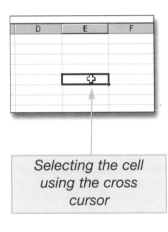

Selecting the cell using the cross cursor

To insert items in a cell:

- The mouse pointer turns into a hollow cross when you move in the spreadsheet. Click the cell you want to fill and it will automatically be surrounded by the selector: a black border in bold face. The cell is now selected.

- Double click inside the cell or in the formula bar to activate the cell.

- Enter the contents of the cell, either directly using the key-board, or indirectly by selecting other cells (as we will explain later).

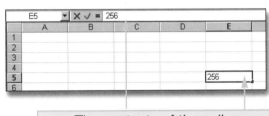

The contents of the cell are displayed in the selected cell and in the formula bar

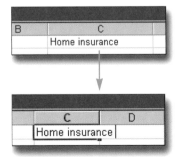

If the contents of a cell exceed its frame, Excel will hide the *overrun*. When you select the cell, its contents will be displayed in full in the formula bar. Cells can be formatted to show the *overrun*.

Selecting a cell range

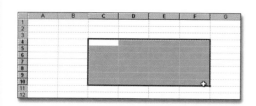

A cell range is a set of continuous cells. To select one, use the drag-and-drop method.

- Click the first cell to select it and keep the left mouse button pressed.
- Drag the mouse pointer to the last cell you want to include in the selection.
- When you have reached that cell, release the button. The selection is made.

Adjacent multiple select

To select several adjacent elements, use the *Shift* key. To select a range of cells, select the first, press *Shift*, keep this key pressed and click the last cell to include in the selection. Proceed in the same way to select several adjacent columns or rows.

Nonadjacent multiple select

Select the items one by one, keeping the *Ctrl* key pressed throughout the operation. With Excel you can select cells, columns or rows, in all combinations, as indicated in the figure on the right.

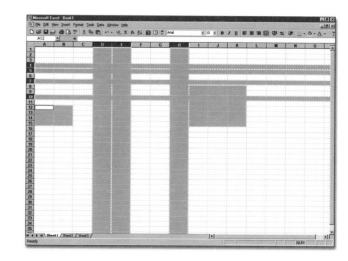

Deselect

To deselect, click outside the selection in the spreadsheet – in an empty cell, for example.

Excel 2000: Introduction

Selecting in Excel 2000

Selecting is an indispensable operation, because that is your way of telling Excel which cells will be edited next. If for example you wish to frame a cell, select it first, then open the border management dialogue box. In Excel you can select nearly everything and anything: one or more cells, columns or rows or a range, a spreadsheet, or even all the worksheet area.

To select a cell:

- Place the mouse pointer on the cell you want to select, and click.

- The cell is now framed in bold face with a black square (the fill handle) in the lower right-hand corner.

The cell is selected

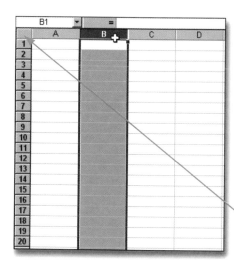

To select a column/row:

- Click the box containing the identifying letter/number.

- The selected cells appear in light grey, except for the first cell which is white.

- All the cells of the column/row are selected (even those that are not displayed on the screen), which means that they will all be affected by the next operation.

Click here to select the entire spreadsheet

- To select the entire active spreadsheet, click in the intersecting box of rows and columns (upper left hand corner).

Sheet1 / Sheet2 / Sheet3 /

Relative and absolute references (2)

If you enter a formula in *E4* to calculate the VAT of the amount in *C3*, Excel will carry out the calculation automatically.

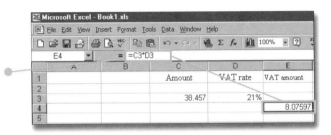

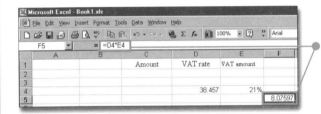

If you move cells, you would expect the reference to produce a wrong result. This does not happen, however, because Excel automatically updates the references and adapts the formula accordingly.

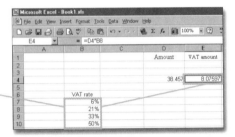

If you refer to an isolated VAT rate in a cell, the formula would give the result shown on the right.

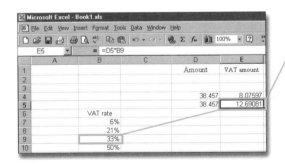

If you copy two cells (Edit/Copy), Excel will update the references and thus produce a wrong result. The amount is multiplied by *B9* (33%), but the VAT rate is still 21%.

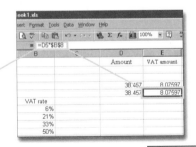

In this case, the reference must be absolute (*C4* or *AZ159*, for example) so that Excel does not adapt the cell reference. To use absolute references, just put the $ in front of each coordinate.

Cell references

Each cell is identified by its reference address, which limits the risk of confusion. Columns have a header composed of letters and rows begin with a number. As there is always only one intersection cell between a row and a column, you simply combine the two to obtain a cell reference. *C3*, for example, is the address of the cell at the intersection of the third row (*3*) and the third column (*C*). Cell *H17* is located at the intersection between the eighth column (*H*) and the seventeenth row (*17*).

Cell addresses range from *A1* to *IV65536*, which means that a spreadsheet contains a maximum of 65536 rows. Column names range from A to Z, then AA to AZ, BA to BZ until IV (the last series commencing with IA), for a total of 256 columns.

The column is named by a letter (A), the row by a number (2), and the cell address by combining these two references (A2).

Relative and absolute references (1)

By default, Excel uses relative references (*C4* or *AZ159* for example), which means that, when you move or copy cells (with the Edit/Copy and Edit/Cut commands), Excel memorises the relationships (cell removal and direction of this removal) between a cell containing a formula and cells containing the data in the formula.

Using templates

A template is a special, preformatted document (it contains predefined format settings). Templates make it easier to produce standard documents such as invoices, purchase orders and expense statements. By using a template, you spare yourself having to format a document (which always takes time, even when you have mastered Excel) and having to enter repetitive headings and information, etc.

To create a new, preformatted workbook:

- Select the File/New command.
- Click the Spreadsheet Solutions tab to display alternative blank spreadsheets (shown on the left).
- Click a template (e.g. Purchase Order) to select it.
- Click OK to confirm.
- The Excel spreadsheet assumes a new form, as shown below)..

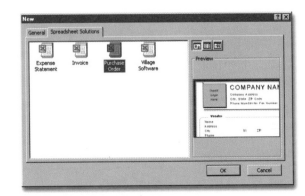

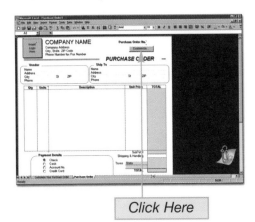

Click Here

To fill the Purchase Order:

- Click the Customise tab to enter your company information (click on Lock/Save Sheet to avoid having to do this again).

- Click the Purchase Order tab and fill in the preformatted document. To fill the headings just click on them (they are hidden cells, but cells nonetheless). Then enter your details (company name, etc.) and the customer's.

File / Save

View / Zoom

Excel 2000: File / New

Creating a new workbook

The workbook is the basic unit in Excel. It is divided into spreadsheets (the work window proper). Each spreadsheet is composed of cells ready to be filled with numbers, text, formulas, etc. When you open Excel, it will display a blank or new '*workbook*.' You can create others at any time. Blank workbooks are not named and are not stored in the computer. They are therefore vulnerable (to power outage, for instance) until they are saved. To view a saved workbook, you must open it (page 14).

To create a new (blank) workbook:

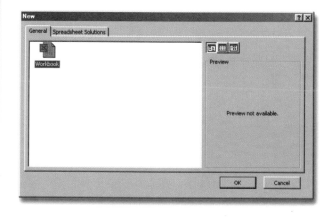

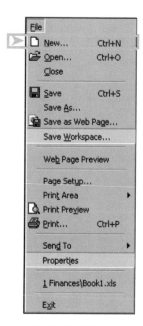

- Click the File/New command.

- Click OK to use the default (Normal) template.

- A blank spreadsheet will be displayed.

- When you create a new workbook it is displayed on top of existing ones. They have not disappeared and are not changed in any way.

File / New

To create a workbook without having to go through the dialogue box presented on this page, press the shortcut keys *Ctrl + N* or click the create document icon (representing a blank sheet).

Automatic opening

The last four workbooks opened are stored by Excel in the lower section of the File menu. Click to open the menu, and then click the folder you want to open.

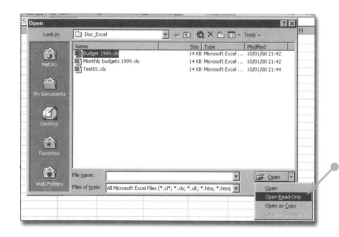

Protected workbook (de facto):

The Open button of the dialogue box contains a drop-down menu with two alternatives for opening a work-book. If you simply click Open, you open a workbook that can be edited (even by error or inadvertently), which, if saved, will update the original on the hard disk.
But, if all you want to do is consult a workbook, just click the down arrow button to open the drop-down menu (as shown on the left) and click Open Read-Only. Excel will not allow you to edit or save the document, so nothing can go wrong.

To open a copy:

Another alternative is to open a copy of a workbook: In this way, any changes made to the copy will not be passed on the the original. The copy will be saved automatically in the same folder as the original but under another name, as if you used the Save As command.

File / Save

File / Save As

File / Close

14

15

Sheet1 / Sheet2 / Sheet3 /

Opening an existing workbook

When you open a workbook that has already been created, i.e. one which has been saved on the hard disk, Excel displays a copy on the screen and keeps the original on the hard disk as a precaution against any ill-advised operation. You can edit this copy and then save it (at which time it will replace the original). It is absolutely vital to master the flowchart screen that gives access to all the folders and files stored on the hard disk, the network or removable disks. Look in contains a drop-down menu with a list of the storage utilities and peripherals installed, including the Windows My Documents folder. ●

To open a workbook:

- Select File/Open.

- Select its location on the hard disk.

- In the Files of type menu, select All Microsoft Excel Files. Only Excel documents will then be listed.

- Enter a name, or simpler still, select the name of the workbook you want. The selected name appears in the window; if it does not, select another folder (directory).

- Click Open to display the workbook on the screen.

By default, Excel stores workbooks in the My Documents folder, which you can open by clicking it.

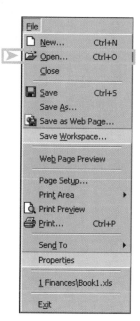

My documents

Open

File management window

File/Open

Ctrl + O

File management dialogue box

This dialogue box makes it easier to manage files by providing all the tools needed to save and arrange them. It is used by several commands, beginning with *Open* and *Save.*

This window shows the contents of the file displayed in the Look in or Save in window. It may contain folders, files or both, depending on how the PC is organised. The drop-down menu gives access to all the 'cabinets' of the computer (hard disk, floppy disk drive, CD-ROM drive) as well as to particular folders (My Documents, for instance). The contents of the cabinet selected here are displayed in the window. To open a file on a floppy disk, for example, click the drop-down menu arrow and click the floppy disk drive.

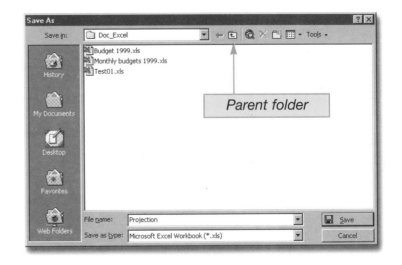

Parent folder

If the workbook you want is in a subfolder, double click this subfolder to open it from the window. If you open a subfolder by mistake, you can go back by clicking on the Parent Folder icon. The left arrow is used to return to the previous screen.

The 'Previous' (left) and 'Parent Folder' icons (right)

File / New

Excel 2000: File / Save

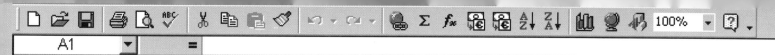

Saving a workbook

If a power cut should occur, you will lose all unsaved data. One of the first things to do with a new workbook is to save it. Give files easily identifiable names so you can find them later. Excel saves files in an orderly manner on the hard disk, where you can subsequently find files and work on them. Excel will open a copy of the workbook and keep the original intact on the hard disk. Make sure you save your work every fifteen minutes or so to keep your workbook regularly updated.

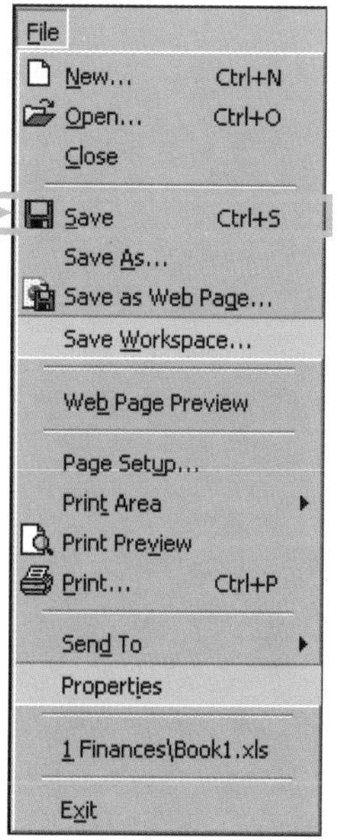

To save a workbook:

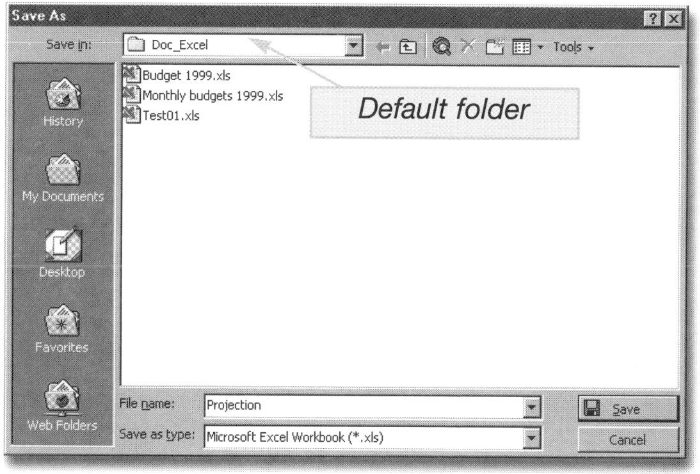

- Select File/Save.
- Select the drive (Save As) and the folder (directory) of the new workbook.
- Enter the name of the file (its reference) in the File name field. Do not exceed 255 characters (avoid \ / . ; * < > : ? " " and the vertical bar).
- Define the type of file (an Excel workbook by default).
- Click Save. The file is placed in the list under the name you have given it. To find it again, open this folder and click on the name of the file to select it.

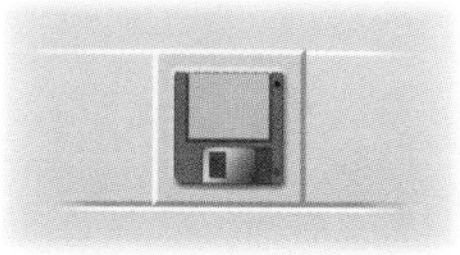

File / Save

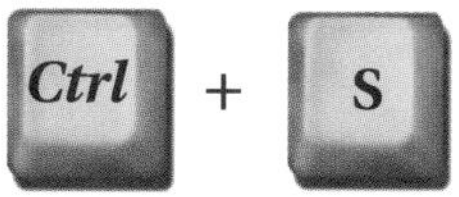

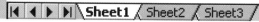

Protecting a workbook

Excel protects a workbook by asking you to enter a password when you open it. You must define this password in the Save As dialogue box. Select File/Save As to begin.

- Click Tools, and then General Options.

- In the Password to open box enter your password. Excel makes a distinction between upper and lower case characters. Do not forget the password you enter, otherwise you will never be able to open the workbook again. Excel automatically hides the characters with asterisks (*).

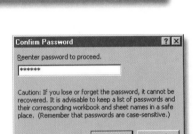

- Click OK. Excel will ask you to Confirm password. Enter the password and click OK. The two dialogue boxes will disappear from the screen.

- Click OK to save the workbook under the same name. Excel will display a warning window telling you that a workbook of that name already exists. This is normal and you should not be alarmed: you can replace it with the same – but protected – version.

- The password must be entered each time you open the protected workbook. If the password you enter is not correct, Excel will cancel the workbook loading operation.

File / New

File / Save

Saving a workbook in another location

On the preceding double page, we discussed how to save new workbooks. This operation can be used in other cases too. For instance, to update the original stored on the hard disk, once you have opened it and made changes (bear in mind that Excel always opens a copy to protect the original against power outage), you can just click the save icon and it will be automatically updated. Or you might want to save your workbook in another folder or under another name, in which case use the File/Save As command to save the copy on the screen (the original is not changed).

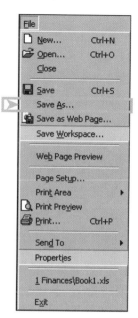

- Select the drive (under Save As) and the host folder of the workbook. You can also select another drive.

- Type the name of the file in the File Name field. You can also enter a new name.

- Define the type of file (Save as Type).

- Click Save.

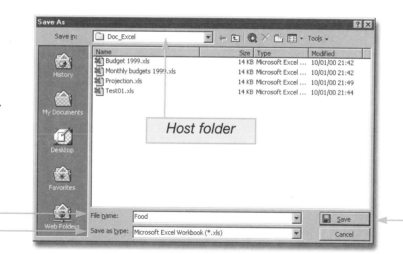

Host folder

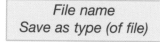

File name
Save as type (of file)

Save
button

You now have two workbooks with the same contents but different names.

A1 ▼ =

Creating a header

The Header/Footer tab is used to define the headers and footers that are to be printed at the top and bottom of each page. They contain information on the workbook (date, author, etc.), or on the originator (particulars, etc.).

To prepare a preset header:

- Click File/Page Setup and click the Header/Footer tab.
- In the Header drop-down menu, select the wording to display in the header.
- The selected wording is displayed in the box above the menu.
- Do the same for the footer (if you want to insert one).
- Click OK.

The header never appears in the spreadsheet. You can, however, see what it will look like when printed with the File/Print Preview command.

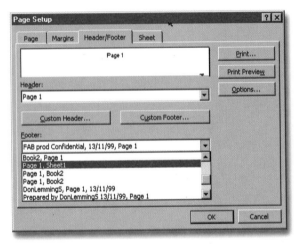

| File / Print Preview |

| File / Print |

| View / Page Break Preview |

To customise a header, click the Custom Header button. Excel displays a new dialogue box entitled Header. This box comprises three zones and various icons that insert fields automatically (data updated automatically such as the print date, for example, not a fixed date). Click OK to return to the previous screen.

Excel 2000 : File / Page Setup

Page setup

The File/Page Setup command defines the position and space that cells will occupy on the printed pages. In it you can set the margins (blank space between the edge of the sheet and the printed worksheet), the scaling (normal size, enlargement or reduction), the headers and footers (two areas situated at the top and bottom of the page that usually contain information on the document or the originator), and the layout and print quality of the page.

To edit the settings of the printed page:

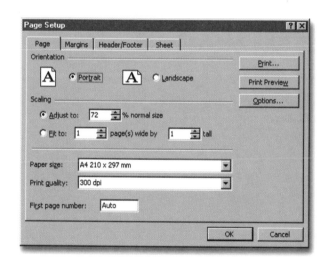

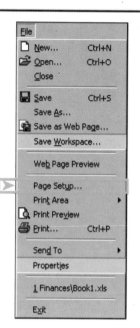

- Select the File/Page Setup command.
- Choose the orientation: portrait (vertical) or landscape (horizontal).
- Select the scaling to print the spreadsheet on a single page. See also the View/Page Break Preview command.
- Select the paper size.
- Select the print quality (determined by the printer).
- Define the page numbering by entering the first page number.
- Click OK.

Use the Margins tab to define the print margins. The default margins will usually suffice for the data to print.

Setting a print area

You do not have to print the entire spreadsheet if all you want is one table. On the contrary, you can select an area and ask Excel to print only this selection. Excel stores your selection in memory, and when you click Print Preview, only this area will be displayed.

To set an area:

- Select the area with the mouse (as you would a range of cells).
- Run the File/Print Area/Set Print Area command.
- Excel keeps the area stored in memory.
- If you then click Print, Excel will print only the selected area.
- To cancel the setting of this area and return to a global, more standard operation, click File/Print Area/Clear Print Area.

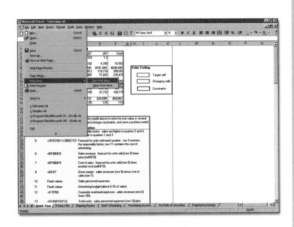

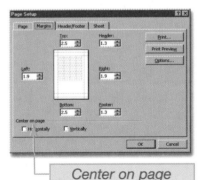

Center on page

To centre a spreadsheet on page:

To centre a spreadsheet on the printed page, select File/Setup. Click the Margins tab, and in the Center on Page header tick Horizontally or Vertically to centre the spreadsheet accordingly. The sheet shown in the centre of the window will adjust to these changes.

View / Page Break Preview

File / Print

File / Page Setup

22

23

Excel 2000 : File / Print Preview

Preparing to print a spreadsheet

In the Print Preview mode, Excel shows the different worksheets as they will be printed. Any headers and/or footers you have defined will also be shown. Cell contents cannot be edited in this mode, but you can go back to the spreadsheet by clicking the Close button.

Click the File/Print Preview command:

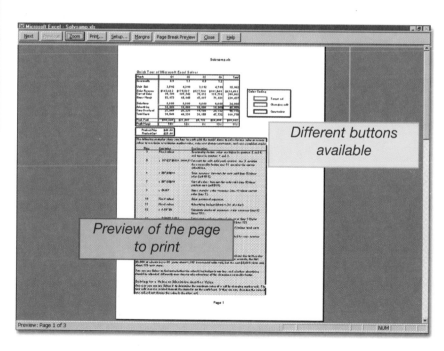

Different buttons available

Preview of the page to print

- Use the Next and Previous buttons to browse and scroll the pages to print.

- To enlarge the page you want to print, click Zoom.

- To access the page settings, click the Page button; the Page Setup dialogue box will appear.

- The Margins button shows or hides the margins as dotted lines on the sheets. You can move these lines by dragging them with the mouse in the Print Preview window.

- The Page Break Preview displays the sheets in the special page break mode.

File / Print Preview

Viewing page breaks

Page breaks are marks inserted by Excel to indicate a new page. These breaks vary depending on the margins and the orientation of the paper. To display them, select View/Page Break Preview. The window now shows blue rectangles with the page numbers (in grey) in the centre.

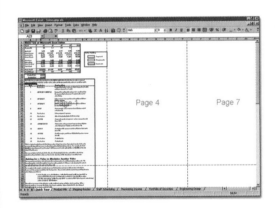

To move page breaks:

To fit an entire worksheet within a single page if some cells overrun to the next page, you must use the mouse. Click the edge of the page to move it. The pointer turns into a double black arrow. Drag the edge (a greyed line gives a preview of the edge location) until the entire spreadsheet is included. Although it looks as if the size of the page has changed, what has actually changed is the scaling for printing. You can check this in File/Page Setup/Page.

To insert a page break:

To insert a page break manually, place the selector in a cell and click Insert/Page Break. The page break will be inserted above the selected cell.

File / Page Setup	File / Print Preview	File / Print area

Printing a spreadsheet

Once you have previewed the sheets (as they will be printed) in Print Preview, you can send the document to the printer. Make sure the printer is switched on and properly connected to the computer and that there is paper in the tray.

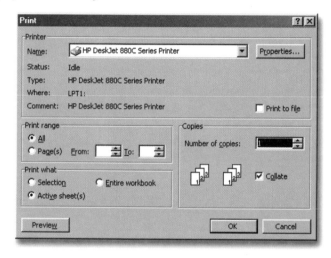

To print a spreadsheet:

- Select File/Print.

- Click the Name field arrow to select the printer from the list. This option is valid only if you have installed several printers with Windows 98.

- In the Print range indicate what you want to print: a range of selected cells, the active sheet(s), or all the sheets of the workbook.

- Enter a number other than '1' in the Number of copies field if you want more than one copy of the same spreadsheet. In this case, you can indicate to Excel the precise printing order (tick the Collate option to print the entire spreadsheet, then a second, etc.).

- If the table extends to several pages, you can indicate the numbers to print by clicking the Page(s) button and entering the page numbers in the From and To fields.

- Now click OK to print.

File / Print

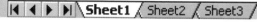

Exiting Excel

When you exit Excel, you carry out the same type of operation as when you close a workbook. The entire program disappears from the screen, leaving even more RAM free (to the benefit of other programs that also need RAM). Excel checks whether all the open workbooks were saved before closing and, if they weren't, will display a warning dialogue box.

To minimise windows:

Numerous dialogue boxes contain *Resize* buttons to specify the scope of a heading or an operation. The File/Page Setup dialogue box, for example, contains such buttons to select the print area, so you no longer have to exit the dialogue box in order to select cells directly in the worksheet. You simply press the appropriate *Resize* button.

When you click a *Resize* button, the dialogue box turns into a floating tool bar and leaves room for the spreadsheet. Select the cells you want with the mouse. To return to the dialogue box, just click the *Restore* button in the floating toolbar.

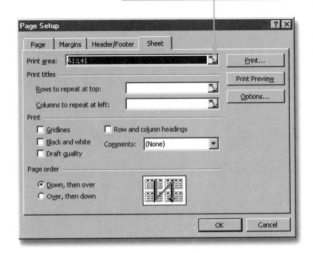

Minimise button

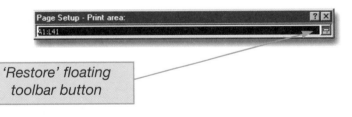

'Restore' floating toolbar button

File / Save

File / Open

Excel 2000 : File / Close

Sheet1 / Sheet2 / Sheet3

Closing a workbook

When you have finished editing or viewing a workbook, close it in order to free valuable memory. Closing the workbook entails closing the screen. The workbook remains on the hard disk and you can retrieve it again whenever you want.

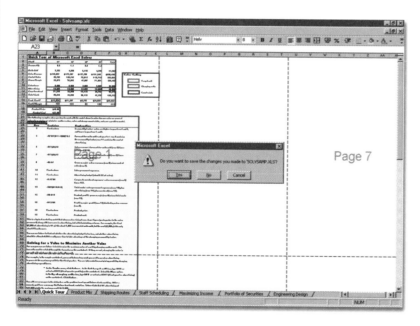

To close a workbook:

- Run the File/Close command.

- If no changes were made to the data since last saved, the workbook will disappear from the screen but remain stored on the hard disk. You can open it whenever you want.

- If the data has been changed since last saved, Excel will not close the workbook automatically, but will display a warning dialogue box first (shown on the left).

- Click Yes to save the changes and close the workbook.

- Click No to close the workbook without saving the changes.

- Click Cancel to cancel the closing operation. The workbook will remain on the screen; the changes, however, will not be saved.

Irreversible operations

Some operations cannot be undone. They relate to file management: open, close, save, print, etc. Excel starts the list again after every save, because it cannot backtrack. Quite surprisingly, Undo is not an irreversible operation.

To redo an operation:

Operations undone via the drop-down menu are automatically emptied into the neighbouring drop-down menu (on the right): the redo menu. It functions exactly as the undo menu, but in the opposite direction, i.e. it restores undone operations. Click the arrow to select the operation to redo. All subsequent operations will also be restored.

To repeat an operation:

The Edit/Repeat command repeats the effect of the last operation in the cell of your choice. 'Last operation' also means last 'dialogue box opened', even if you have changed dozens of settings in it. For cell formatting purposes, Excel suggests that you get round this by using the Reproduce format tool.

Reproduce format

Edit / Repeat

Ctrl + Y

Excel 2000: Edit / Undo

Undoing an operation

Anyone can make a wrong move in Excel. But Excel 2000 will always allow you to undo the last operation you carried out. The Edit/Undo command cancels the effect of the preceding operation (text deleted inadvertently for instance). To run this command, simply click the Edit menu and then Undo.

But that's not all: Excel keeps track of all the operations carried out since the beginning of the session and puts them in a list.

To undo several operations:

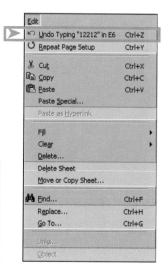

• Click the arrow to the right of the Undo icon.

• The list of the last operations carried out is displayed.

• Just indicate the operation you wish to undo, and click on it. However, be careful: When you undo one operation, the program will automatically undo ALL SUBSEQUENT OPERATIONS.

• The list status bar indicates the number of operations undone when you click in the list (this number changes with the selected operation to undo).

A combination of keys produces the same result:
The keys shortcut *Ctrl* + *Z*. If there is one shortcut to learn by heart, then this is it. Don't forget: if you make a mistake press *Ctrl* + *Z* and the mistake is undone!

Edit / Undo

The Clipboard

A new innovation in Excel 2000 is the multiple clipboard, which allows you to keep up to twelve different items at any one time. The capacity of the Clipboard is unlimited: it accepts any type of data including text, formulas, images, sounds and video clips. As in all programs, it can be used to easily import images to Excel, or conversely, to export Excel data or graphics to Word or PowerPoint.

There is no limit to how long an item can be kept in the Clipboard. It is emptied when you turn off the computer. Once the clipboard has twelve items it is full and so when you enter a thirteenth, this will replace the first item and a fourteenth will replace the second item, and so on.

You can display the contents of the Clipboard with the View/Toolbars/Clipboard command.
By default, you will paste the last selection sent to the Clipboard. Just click on another selection
to insert it at the selector location.

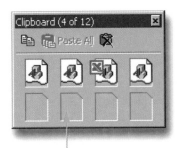

The different files contained
in the Clipboard

The locations occupied are represented by an icon, which varies depending on the nature of the stored item. To display the contents of each memory, point at one and wait: a bubble appears displaying the 'cut' or 'copied' selection.

Edit / Paste

Edit / Paste special

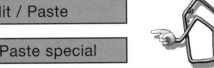

Sheet1 / Sheet2 / Sheet3

Excel 2000 : Edit / Cut / Copy

Moving and copying items

In Excel 2000, you can move or copy a selection without difficulty, the way you would using a pair of scissors and a tube of glue. Indeed, we even talk of cut, copy and paste (see page 32). Cutting a selection consists of extracting it from the image and placing it in a special memory, a Windows facility shared by all the programs: the Clipboard. Pasting a selection entails finding it in the Clipboard and reinserting it in a program. The Copy command sends a clone of the selection to the Clipboard. It does not extract it but simply makes a copy, so when the selection is pasted, it will appear in two copies in the spreadsheet.

To move a selection:

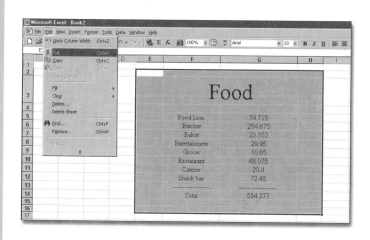

- Select the block of cells to move.

- Run the Edit/Cut command. Excel displays the block within a dashed line.

- Place the selector at the location of destination.

- Select Edit/Paste (see next pages). Excel will make the blocks of cells appear where you have selected.

Edit / Cut

Edit / Copy

To copy a selection, proceed in exactly the same way, but with the Edit/Copy command. The selection will be copied (not cut).

Drag and drop

If you prefer to work with a mouse to move an item, select it, click on its frame (the external edges of the selection), and keep the mouse button pressed. Now drag the selection to another location. When you have reached the point you want, release the mouse button. The selection appears. To copy an item, proceed in the same way keeping the *Alt* key pressed.

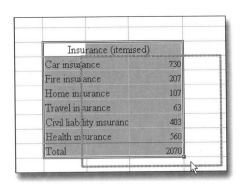

Paste special:

The Edit/Paste Special command is available for the last selection cut or copied. It is used to copy particular characteristics of the selection, such as the contents, edges, formula, etc. Click on the destination cell to activate it. Select Edit/Paste Special. The dialogue box opened will vary depending on the nature of the pasted item. A simple cell containing a formula displays an option window. Tick the items to paste (upper part) or the type of operation to carry out (lower part of the window). If you click Paste Link, you create a link between the cell of origin and the destination cell. Any change to the former will be passed on to the latter.

Click OK to confirm the options of your Paste Special

Edit / Cut

Edit / Copy

Excel 2000 : Edit / Paste

Inserting items

If you run the Edit/Paste command, Excel will paste into the active spreadsheet the last selection copied or cut in the Clipboard. You can thus paste an infinite number of identical selections into one or more spreadsheets. To access the other items stored in the Clipboard, you must first display it.

To insert an item stored in the Clipboard into the workbook:

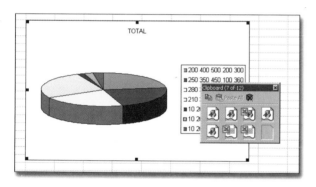

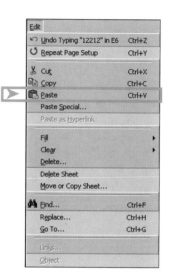

- Click the cell where you want to paste an item from the clip-board. It will be framed by the selector (a black rectangle).

- To view the contents of the Clipboard, select View/Toolbars/Clipboard.

- Locate the selection to insert by passing over each item with the mouse and waiting for its contents to be displayed in a bubble.

- Click the item to insert.

To insert the last item stored, run the Edit/Paste command. In the screenshot on the left, a pie chart has been pasted into the workbook.

Edit / Paste

If you move the block of cells onto cells containing data, Excel will display a warning message before overwriting the data. To undo the operation, click the Undo button. To confirm, click OK.

Types of series

Date: based on dates and times; enter the first value, and Excel will continue the series. If you enter *Monday* (*1:00*) in the first cell, Excel will display *Tuesday* (*2:00*), *Wednesday* (*3:00*), etc., in the subsequent cells.

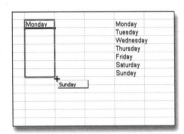

Date

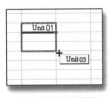

AutoFill

AutoFill: composed of a character string and an indexed number, this series accepts such expressions as *Quarter 1* (*Quarter 2*, *Quarter 3*, etc.).

Growth: Excel 2000 multiplies the items of the series by a constant value. If you enter *1* and *3* as initial values, Excel will display *9, 27, 81, 243* in the subsequent cells.

To create a complex series:

- Enter the first item of the series.
- Enter the Fill Handle and create a selection by dragging the mouse pointer down and releasing it when the number of selected cells corresponds to the number of items you want in the series.
- Run Edit/Fill/Series.
- Select the type of series with one of the buttons in the Type area.
- Enter a number in the Step value field. A step is the interval between two values of the series. This information is necessary, because a single value was provided as the starting point for the series.
- Click OK to confirm.

Edit / Copy

Tools / Options / Custom Lists

34

Creating automatic lists

Edit / Fill / Series

In Excel, logical lists such as the days of the week, the months, a series of numbers (1, 2, 3, 4) etc. are used quite often. Thanks to Excel, you no longer need to strain your fingers typing all the items on the list: just enter the first two, then draw a rectangle using the mouse. The program will complete the list until it reaches the last selected cell. The series corresponds to an indexed series of numbers or expressions (dates, times, character strings) that are part of the same family.

For a simple series:

① Enter the first two items of the series: *1* and *5* for example.

② Click the two cells.

③ Click the Fill Handle (the black square in the lower right corner of the selector). Excel changes the mouse pointer into a black cross.

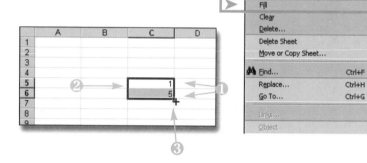

④ Keep the mouse button pressed and drag the pointer down. A bubble displays the value of the current item depending on the basic values of the series.

⑤ Release the mouse button to view the different items entered by the spreadsheet.

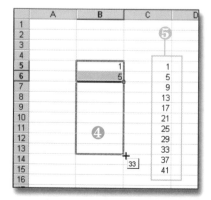

> **Note:** The default series is linear:
>
> Excel adds (or subtracts) a constant to the different items of the series. In our example Excel adds 4 (5 minus 1).

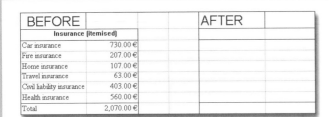

Edit/Delete/Content (*Del*):

You can delete the contents of a cell by simply pressing the *Del* key. First click the cell to display the selector then press *Del*. Excel immediately erases the data and leaves the selector on the cell in case you want to enter new data. This *Del* key is the shortcut to the Edit/Delete/Content command.

Edit/Delete/Format:

Excel can delete all the formatting attributes of a cell, including background colour, pattern, orientation, colour, size and fonts, etc., in a single operation.

To delete the format

- Select the cell or range of cells whose format you want to delete.
- Click Edit/Delete/Format.
- It's done. The operation is irreversible.

To delete a spreadsheet:

To delete an entire spreadsheet, use the Edit/Delete sheet command. Excel asks you to confirm, because this operation is irreversible. Notice that the message comes from the *Office Assistant* when activated.

Edit / Cut

Edit / Undo

Sheet1 / Sheet2 / Sheet3

Excel 2000 : Edit / Delete

Deleting items

To delete entire rows, columns or pages of cells, you use the **Edit/Delete** command. During the deletion operation, Excel automatically shifts cells up (or to the left) so as not to leave any rows (or columns) empty. If you delete a column, Excel automatically changes the structure of the table and shifts all the columns one notch to the left, without going through the dialogue box. The data of column *E* is now in *D*, for example, which causes no problem for the formulas, because Excel updates the references.

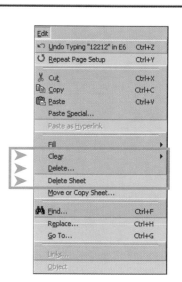

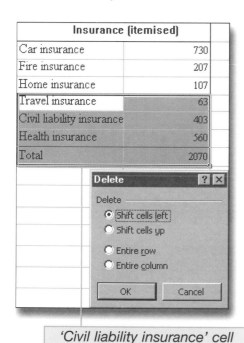

If you do not select an entire column but only a few cells, Excel gives you a shift option.

- Select a range of cells.

- Run Edit/Delete to display the dialogue box.

- Click Shift cells up and then click OK. Excel deletes the contents of the cells. Only the 'Civil liability insurance' cell and those below it are shifted.

> **Warning:** if you do not select an entire column and click the *Shift cells left* option, you may obtain an incomprehensible spreadsheet.

'Civil liability insurance' cell and lower cells are selected

To name a sheet:

Names like *Sheet1* give no indication as to what the sheet contains. Depending on the data entered, you will want to customise the sheet tabs.

To rename a sheet:

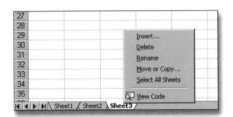

- Click the tab with the right-hand mouse button to display a shortcut menu.
- Click Rename.
- In the two boxes, Excel displays the name in reverse video and a blinking cursor in the tab.
- Enter the new name. The former name is deleted automatically.
- When you have entered the new name, press Enter to confirm.

To add a sheet:

- Click the tab of the sheet in front of which you want to add a new sheet.
- Select Insert/Worksheet. Excel will automatically add a new sheet in front of the one displayed on the screen. The spreadsheet always uses the same numbering sequence to name the sheet: if three unnamed sheets were in the workbook, the new sheet would be named *Sheet4*.

Edit / Delete sheet

Format / Sheet

To navigate:

Four buttons can be used to navigate in the sheet. From left to right, these are:

To the first sheet in the workbook; To the left in the area;
To the right in the area; To the last sheet in the workbook.

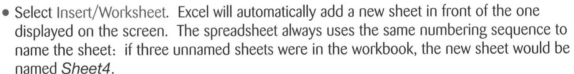

Excel 2000 : Edit / Move or copy sheet

Managing spreadsheets

All workbooks consist of three default spreadsheets: Sheet1, Sheet2 and Sheet3. To access the data in each of them, simply click on the respective tab. The name of the active spreadsheet (the one displayed) appears in bold face. Excel allows you up to 255 spreadsheets per workbook, and you can interchange the positions of the sheets at all times.

To move a sheet:

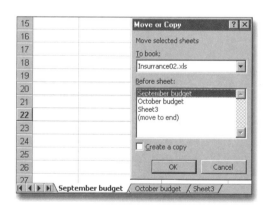

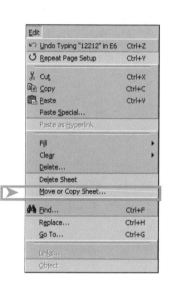

- Select the sheet(s) to move and select Edit/Move or Copy Sheet.

- The To book heading displays a drop-down menu with the list of open workbooks.

- Click a workbook to tell Excel it is the destination workbook for the selected sheets.

- Under Before Sheet, select the target location, i.e. the sheet prior to where you want to place the moved sheet.

- Click OK to confirm.

To copy a sheet, follow the procedure described above, and tick Create a copy before you click OK.

To replace a character string:

- Select Edit/Replace.
- In the Find what field, enter or paste the character string you want to replace.
- In the Replace with field, enter or paste the replacement string.
- Select the direction of the search: By Rows or By Columns.
- Tick the necessary options.
- Click Find Next to go to the next occurrence of the string in the spreadsheet without replacing it.
- Click Replace to replace this occurrence (which is selected automatically by Excel in the datasheet).
- Click Replace All to automatically replace all occurrences.
- Click Close when the necessary replacements have been carried out.

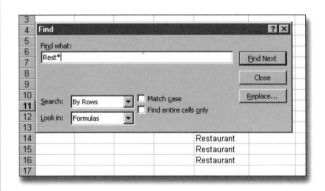

Wildcard characters:

The characters ? and * are wildcards that can replace any character ('?') and any character string ('*'). If you are not sure about two similar words, use the '*' wildcard and enter, for example conn* in the Find what field. Excel will stop on 'connect' and 'connection' (but also on 'connector' etc.). Similarly, if you conduct your search with 'm?re', Excel will stop on 'more,' 'mere,' 'mare,' etc., but not on 'maure' or 'merit.'

Edit / Replace

Find-Replace a character string

Find is one of the most standard commands in the IT world, indispensable for finding a precise item in a text, spreadsheet or multi-page presentation. Type a word or just a few letters (or figures) and ask Excel to find it in the spreadsheet. This command is accompanied by the Replace function, whereby you can tell Excel to replace the word sought systematically without verifying each occurrence. Excel asks you to specify a search area by selecting it. If you don't select a search area, it will carry out the search on the entire spreadsheet.

To find a character string:

- Select Edit/Find.

- In the Find what field, type or paste the character string you want to find.

- Select the search direction: By Rows or By Columns.

- Select the type of item: the values (the default setting, which forces Excel to check the content of the cells) or by Formulas.

- Tick the necessary options.

- Click Next to go to the next occurrence of the word in the spreadsheet.

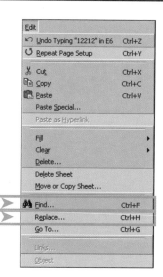

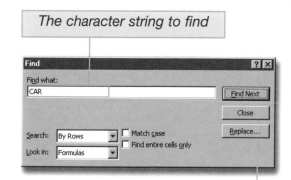

The character string to find

The Replace button is described in detail on the next page

Edit/Find

Ctrl + F

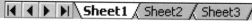

Toolbar management (continued)

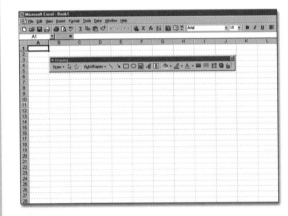

You can move toolbars three ways: from the spreadsheet (where they are floating) to a side of the screen (where they are fixed); from one side of the screen to a spreadsheet; or within the spreadsheet itself.

To move a fixed toolbar (under the menu bar, for example) in the spreadsheet, proceed as follows:

- Click the vertical bar on the left of the toolbar and keep the left mouse button pressed.

- Move the mouse to the desired location.

- Release the left mouse button.

To change the form of toolbar, click on one side. A double arrow pointer appears. Click and, keeping the mouse button pressed, stretch or condense the toolbar.

To hide a floating toolbar, click the close button (the cross, on the right in the title bar).

A toolbar has disappeared:

Click the View/Toolbars command, if one or more toolbars have disappeared from the screen after an inadvertent click or a command confirmed by mistake. The toolbar should reappear intact.

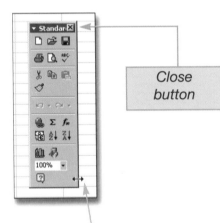

Close button

Horizontal, two-headed arrow button

Excel 2000 : View / Toolbar

Toolbar management

Excel has developed a command code that is easy to learn. It uses icons (small images at the top of the screen) which appear as buttons with a picture symbolising a standard command. The yellow folder symbolises, for instance, the opening of a workbook; the small disk represents the File/Save command; the pair of scissors the Edit/Cut command, and so on. This means you do not need to go through the menus: just click on an icon to carry out the corresponding operation. The icons are grouped by topic, and each 'pack' of icons is called a 'toolbar'. Excel has 17 'floating' tool bars (which can be hidden when you want).

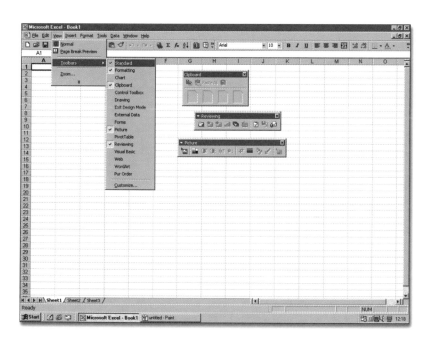

To display a toolbar:

- Excel 2000 shows three toolbars by default: the *standard toolbar* (basic file management functions: open, print, etc.), the *formatting toolbar* (containing the formatting commands) and the *Euroview toolbar* (which converts values into euros).

- To view one or more additional toolbars, run View/Toolbars.

- Wait for the submenu to be displayed.

- Click the toolbar of your choice. The menu disappears.

- This toolbar is displayed in the middle of the screen and can be moved as necessary.

To insert a comment:

First select the cell(s) in which you want to insert the comment. Click the right mouse button, and select Insert comment (or run the Insert/Comment command). A box appears containing the name of the originator of the comment (you). Enter a comment. When you have finished, click outside the box to exit. The box disappears.

	Amount	Deduction	LemmingS: Justify such a deduction %
Car insurance	500	54%	
Coffee	125	100%	
Restaurant	250	30%	
Restaurant	311	30%	
Restaurant	238	30%	

To edit a comment:

To edit a comment, select the cell to which it applies and click the right mouse button. Run the Edit comment command. The yellow box appears and you can now edit the comment. To change the appearance of the comment, select it and use the Format/Comment command. Change the settings as indicated in the Format/Cell section.

To review comments:

To review a comment, activate the Review toolbar. The icons, from left to right, are used to edit the active comment; go to the next comment, hide the comment, hide all comments and, very important, delete the active comment (without confirmation).

Insert / Comments	View / Toolbars / Review	Format / Cell

Sheet1	Sheet2	Sheet3

Excel 2000 : View/ Comment

Viewing comments

Comments inserted in Excel resemble the yellow *Post-it* form. When hidden, the presence of a comment in a cell is indicated by a red triangle in the upper right corner of that cell. Comments are generally entered by a user as reminders or by a colleague who is revising the spreadsheet and the data it contains. It is useful to be able to review the comments with ease, so Excel has dedicated a tool for this purpose: the Review toolbar.

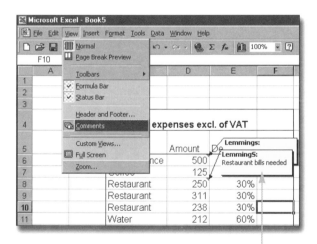

Comment are displayed in yellow Post-it® form

To view the comments:

The View/Comments command is a toggle command. When the icon is pressed, all the comments are displayed. When it is not pressed, they are all hidden.

To display a comment on a cell, press the mouse cursor gently. The comment appears a few seconds later.

To hide comments:

To hide all the comments and display only the red triangles, click View/Comments a second time. The second click cancels the effect of the first.

Items have disappeared:

Anything can happen in computing. For instance, what happens if an item usually displayed constantly disappears (formula bar, scroll bars, etc.)? In such a case, have a look at the options ticked in the Tools/Options dialogue box, and more precisely in the View tab. It contains numerous options. The ticked items are obviously displayed, whereas the others are not. Make sure that the items you require are duly ticked (the row and column headers, workbook or formula bar tabs, for example).

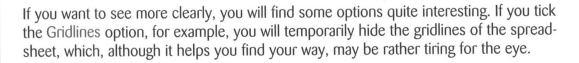

To edit the view:

If you want to see more clearly, you will find some options quite interesting. If you tick the Gridlines option, for example, you will temporarily hide the gridlines of the spreadsheet, which, although it helps you find your way, may be rather tiring for the eye.

To view formulas:

By default, Excel calculates the result of formulas automatically and displays it in the appropriate cells. The formula is displayed in the formula bar if the cell is selected. To display it in the cell, tick Formulas. Untick afterwards.

Tools / Options / View

ENLARGING THE VIEW

The default zoom value is 100%. To enlarge part of the spreadsheet, increase this value to 150 or 200%. Conversely, for an overall view of the entire sheet, reduce the zoom to 25% or 50%. You can zoom in on a selection too. In this case, the selection occupies the entire screen.

To change the zoom value:

- Select View/Zoom.

- Select a preset zoom value by ticking the corresponding box with the mouse.

- Click OK to confirm.

Ref.	Type	Amount	Total VAT excl.	VAT rate	Global VAT	De
	Shoes (John)	12	720.00 €	21%	871.20 €	
	John's wedding	1	3,000.00 €	6%	3,630.00 €	
	Lotto	54	108.00 €	21%	130.68 €	
	Gifts for Jules and Jim	14	779.00 €	21%	942.59 €	
	Mike' passport	1	32.00 €	21%	38.72 €	
	Jumper	4	5.80 €	21%	7.02 €	
	Bag	6	412.00 €	21%	498.52 €	
	PC	3	3,865.00 €	21%	4,676.65 €	
	Car insurance	1	730.00 €	21%	883.30 €	
	Fire insurance	1	207.00 €	21%	250.47 €	
	Home insurance	1	107.00 €	21%	129.47 €	
	Travel insurance	1	63.00 €	21%	76.23 €	100%
	Civil liability insurance	1	403.00 €	21%	487.63 €	100%
	Health insurance	1	560.00 €	21%	677.60 €	100%

Excel offers three categories of zoom values:

- *Default scales (200%, 100%, etc.)*
- *Zoom to fit the selection.*
- *Custom zoom.*

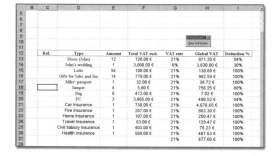

Excel features a direct zoom: the drop-down menu built in the standard toolbar. Click the arrow to invoke it and select a value.

To make the most of the screen's capacity, use the View/Full Screen command. Excel will then hide all superfluous items (toolbars, formula bar, Windows taskbar) to make maximum room for the data. The view size depends on the value you have given to the zoom. To exit this mode, click the Close full screen button in the Full Screen floating toolbar.

To insert rows or columns:

- Select the adjacent item in the table. A row will be inserted above the selected row; a column to the left of the selected column. You are not required to select the item corresponding to the one you wish to insert. You can choose to insert only one cell.

- Select Insert/Item. The selected item is inserted.

To insert several rows (or several columns):

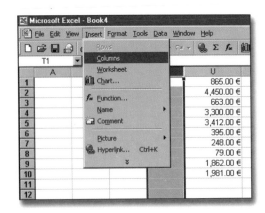

- Select as many items as you want to insert. To insert three rows, for example, select three rows (here: 23, 24 and 25). To insert one cell, select one cell. To insert four, select four etc.

- Confirm the Insert/Item command.

- Excel will insert as many items as have been selected.

20		
21	Food	74.725
22	Butcher	254.875
23		
24		
25		
26	Baker	23.152
27	Entertainment	29.95
28	Grocer	10.65
29	Restaurant	48.075
30	Caterer	20.4
31	Snack bar	72.45
32		
33	Total	534.277
34		
35		

(shortcut menu:)
- Cut
- Copy
- Paste
- Paste Special...
- Insert
- Delete
- Clear Contents
- Format Cells...
- Row Height...
- Hide
- Unhide

When you select column T (containing figures), confirm the Insert/Column command. A new column T appears, and the former is shifted one column to the right (and is now called U).

Note:

The shortcut cell menu (right mouse button) also contains the Insert command.

Excel 2000 : Insert / Cells

| A1 | ▼ | = |

Inserting items in a spreadsheet

You can insert a row, a column or a range of cells in a spreadsheet whenever you want. These items are blank and adopt the format of the neighbouring cells (background colour, edges, font type and size, etc.). The Insert menu contains the Cells, Rows and Columns commands you can use to enter items (you may have to pop up the menu to access these three commands).

To insert cells:

- Select the precise number of cells you want to insert.

- Select the Insert/Cells command.

- Excel does not know how to shift the contents of the selected cells so as not to lose information and not to destructure the spreadsheet. So it displays an Insert Cell dialogue box.

- You can use the options to shift cells right or left, or simply to shift an entire row or an entire column.

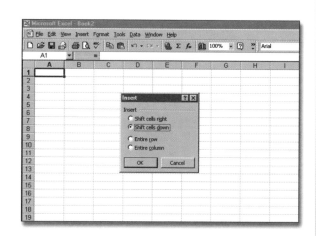

> **Warning:**
> By inserting a few cells, you change the way the spreadsheet is organised, since the rows (or columns) no longer correspond. Enter complete rows or columns rather than 'flying' cells.

- Click OK to confirm the insertion.

Different types of charts

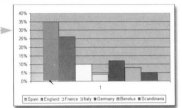

Bar chart

Column chart: Default chart inserted by Graph. A column chart shows how data develops over a specified period. Its main purpose is to enable you to compare items. Categories are arranged horizontally; values vertically.

Bar chart: Used to compare the contribution of each series in relation to a sum of equal values (usually 100%).

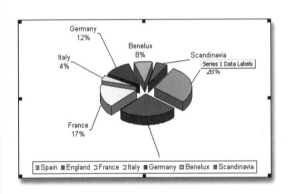

Pie chart

Pie chart: Displays the proportional size of items in relation to the whole. It is limited to displaying a series of data (months or expenses, for example, not both). Ideal for comparing market shares at a given time. Can be created in 3D (it is then possible to separate the pieces of the pie).

Line chart: Unbeatable for viewing the development of each expenditure item in time. Practical, but not very appealing.

Area chart: Displays trends over time.

Radar: Displays all categories and values. Each item has its own value axis originating in the centre of the radar. Analysing this type of chart takes a little getting used to.

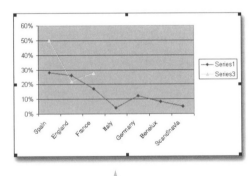

Line chart

Format/ Row (Column) / Hide

Chart Menu

Inserting a chart in the spreadsheet

Charts spare you the effort of reading data fixed in tables by highlighting the most important items in them. To create charts, Excel has a special wizard that uses four dialogue boxes to help you find the most appropriate chart for the type of data you want to highlight. One small, but extremely important detail: all charts are linked to the data of the spreadsheet, so any change of the data automatically updates the chart.

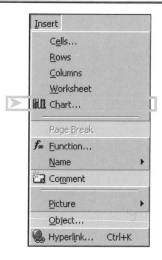

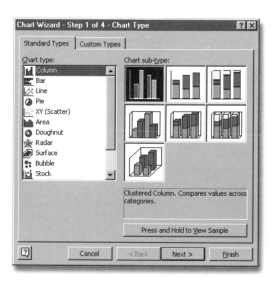

To insert a chart:

- Select the data from the spreadsheet that will be featured in the chart. If necessary, hide certain rows or columns that might create confusion, complicate the chart unneccessarily.

- Click on a type of chart in the Chart type list.

- Do not forget to specify the subtype by clicking one of the charts featured in the Chart sub-type area.

- To view what the chart will look like in the end, press the Press and Hold to View Sample button: it simulates the chart using the data selected in the spreadsheet.

- Click Next to go to *step 2*.

Titles, Axes, Gridlines, Legend

You can use the above to improve the appearance of your chart. The tabs can be used to add titles for the chart and the X and Y axes (Titles tab), labels of values corresponding to data (Data Labels tab); values of X and Y axes (Axes tab); different gridlines according to the X and/or Y axis (Gridlines tab); a legend for the colours used by the different series of data (Legend tab) or a table containing data below the chart (Data Table tab).

Try all these options. You can see what they will look like in the Preview Box and, if you do not like them, you can untick the option, delete the text entered in the text field or tick the default option.

Click Next if you are not satisfied with the way the chart looks.

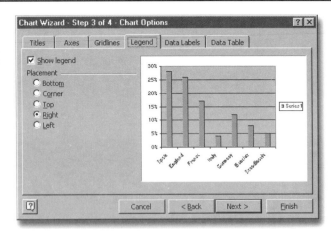

The Legend tab in the Chart Wizard

New sheet or object?

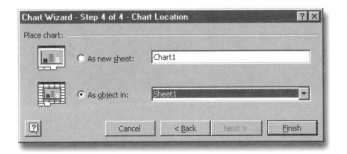

In this last box, you will choose where to insert the chart. By default, it will be inserted as an object on the sheet indicated in the As object in area. To place it in a new sheet, click the As new sheet button and enter the name of the sheet in the corresponding field.

Chart Menu

52

Inserting a chart in a spreadsheet (2)

You must still do three things to insert the chart. In the second dialogue box, choose the data you want to appear in the chart (see p.50). If you have already carried out this task before activating the chart wizard, go directly to the next step. The third dialogue box contains all the worksheet formatting options: Legend, placement, etc. Finally, the last dialogue box suggests that you create the chart either on a new sheet, independent from the workbook, or that you insert it as an object on the spreadsheet in which the worksheet is located.

Let us continue the chart insertion process (*second dialogue box*):

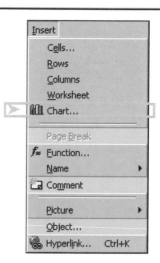

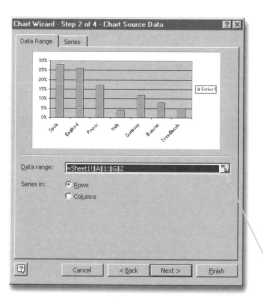

- If you have already selected a worksheet, click Next to go to the second dialogue box.

- Otherwise, use the Minimise button on the far right-hand corner of the Data Range field.

- Select the data you want to display in chart form. To make the dialogue box reappear, just click the Restore button in the floating toolbar.

- You can change the appearance of the chart by changing the reference axes.

- Click Next to continue.

- Click the Series Tab to edit each series of data displayed on the screen.

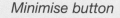

Minimise button

To change the appearance:

To change the characteristics (colour, edges, fonts, number format, alignment, scale, etc.) of a chart item, double click on the item in the chart to display a corresponding Format dialogue box. You can click on the axes and the gridlines, the background and the different constituent elements of the chart. The Format dialogue box of the 'selected item' looks like the Format/Cells dialogue box.

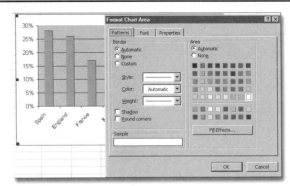

Working with a chart:

A chart inserted in a sheet is an object, unlike a chart created as a new sheet. It can therefore be moved very easily. Before you carry out such operations, you must select the chart areas. Click on the chart, and Excel will display eight black handles which encapsulate your selection.

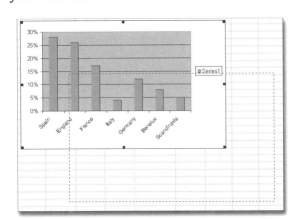

To move a chart:

- Click the object and keep the mouse button pressed. Avoid clicking the chart or a title. Select a blank area of the object.

- Move the mouse pointer to see a ghost of the object's frame move.

- When you have reached the place you want on the sheet, release the mouse button.

54

55

Excel 2000: Insert / Chart / 3D View

A1		=	

Changing the appearance of a chart

The settings selected when you insert a chart are not definitive. You can access every dialogue box from the Chart Menu. The first dialogue box corresponds to the Chart/Chart Type command, and the second relates to the Chart Source data command. The chart options (3rd dialogue box) are grouped under the command of the same name. To change the location of the chart, click Chart/Location. Some charts can be displayed in 3D through a series of adjustable settings.

Chart
- Chart Type...
- Source Data...
- Chart Options...
- Location...
- Add Data...
- Add Trendline...
- 3-D View...

To change the 3D characteristics of a chart:

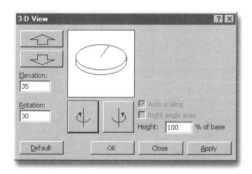

- Click the Chart/3D view command.

- To rotate the chart, enter an angle of rotation in the Rotation field or click the arrows turning round an axis.

- To change the angle of view, change the Elevation or click the arrows above this heading.

Note

When a chart is inserted, a new drop-down menu called Charts appears between the Tools and Windows menus.

- To change the Height/base ratio, enter a new percentage in the Height field (the smaller this percentage, the more 'packed' the chart).

- Click OK to apply these settings (the chart can be previewed in a wire frame).

To define formulas:

A formula is an equation composed of operands (an operand is a constant value entered with the keyboard, the contents of a selected cell, a function, etc.) and operators (+, -, *, /, % or ^ [exponent] for the arithmetic operators producing a numbered result ; <, >, =, >=, <=, <> for comparison operators producing a 'True' or 'False' type of result; etc.). Formulas begin with the equals sign (=) and yield a value.

Examples of formulas:

=2*3.1415*A1 : represents the result of the constant values 2, *Pi* and the numeric value contained in Cell *A1*.

=C2>C3 : this formula displays the logical value *TRUE* if the content of Cell *C2* is greater than the content of the Cell *C3*, and the logical value *FALSE* otherwise.

To insert a formula in a sheet:

- Click in the result sheet to place the selector.
- Click in the formula bar to display the blinking cursor and enter the equals sign '='.
- Indicate the first cell to multiply by clicking on it as if you selected it. Its reference will be displayed in the formula bar and in the cell.
- Type in the multiplication sign (*).
- Identify the second cell whose contents are to be multiplied.
- Press *Enter* to confirm.

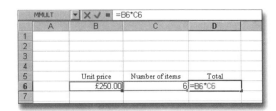

Excel 2000: Insert / Function

A1 =

Inserting an automatic function

Functions are predefined mathematical formulas used to carry out various operations. They contain variables called arguments that must be completed for the function to produce a result. Functions can be inserted in a formula or used separately in a cell. Every function has a different syntax because each one uses specific arguments. All nonetheless follow certain basic rules: they all begin with the equals sign ' = ', followed by the name of the function, open parenthesis ' (', arguments separated by semicolons ' ; ' and close parenthesis ') '. The most current functions are nested in the formula bar.

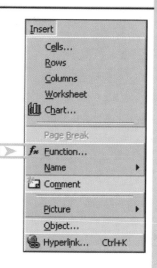

To add a column of figures:

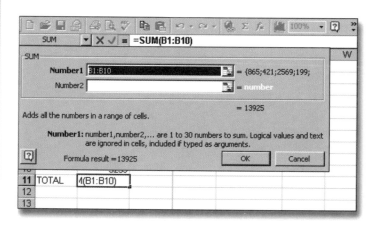

- Select the cell that is to display the sum.

- Enter the equals sign '=' in the formula bar. Excel displays a drop-down menu of the current functions on the left.

- Select the SUM function.

- A dialogue box appears. Minimise it with the 'Number1' button. The spreadsheet is displayed. Select in it the figures you want to add.

- Click the Restore button in the floating toolbar to return to the dialogue box.

- Click OK. The addition result is displayed in the cell selected at the outset.

Excel inserts the function in the formula bar and displays the five fields mentioned on p.58 for you to fill in.

You can enter the values either directly in the appropriate text fields, or minimize the dialogue box by clicking on the icon to select the reference cell in the spreadsheet.

- Click OK to confirm these values.

- The result is displayed in the cell.

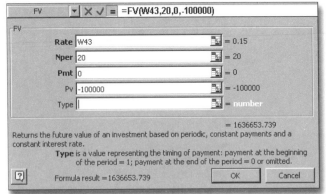

Note 1

An interest rate is expressed as a %, and this percentage is translated into a whole number by Excel.

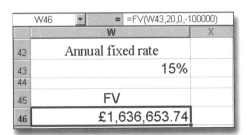

Note 2

The Pmt value is 0: this is normal, because we are not calculating monthly repayments of a sum, for example. We rely on a single payment at the end of ten years.

Note 3

You probably flinched when you saw that the initial capital (*Pv*) shown in the screenshot on the top-right of the page, is negative. This is because the conventions in force in Excel require it however, so don't panic. The money you invest is always represented by a negative number. When you put the money into an account, it is considered 'spent.' Conversely, your revenues and dividends are always positive. If you indicated a positive number in Pv, you would have undoubtedly obtained a result identical to that displayed above, but negative.

Excel 2000: Insert / Function

Inserting a complex financial function

To illustrate this operation, we can evaluate the future value of an investment at a fixed interest rate. For instance, what return would you get from £100,000 deposited within a large Bahamas bank over ten years?

Select a financial function: *FV* (for ' *future value* '). In this case, Excel requests five pieces of data:

❶ Rate: Interest rate in force.

❷ Nper: Number of periods.

❸ Pmt: Fixed payment of return per period.

❹ Pv: Initial capital.

❺ Type: Type of investment, the value of which may be 0 or 1. Enter '1' if payments are due at the beginning of the period. By default, Excel considers that you will be paid at the end of the period (value = 0).

To apply a complex function:

- Select the host cell of the function.

- Click the Insert/Function command or the fx icon. Excel opens the dialogue box shown on the right.

- Choose the function category (in our case, a financial function). All the functions linked to this category are displayed in the right window pane.

- Click the appropriate function in this pane (FV in our case) to select it.

- Click OK to confirm your choice and apply the selected function in the host cell.

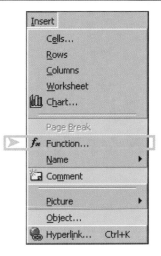

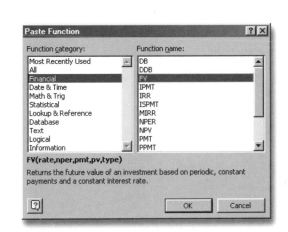

Error!

Excel uses conventions for the errors it encounters.

The result is larger than the host cell. Enlarge the cell or apply a different number format.

#DIV/0! The formula contains a division by zero, which is impossible. Change the cell reference of the divider or change the division value.

#N/A Not/Applicable. The formula refers to an empty cell.

#NAME? Excel does not recognise the text used in the formula.

#NUMBER! A problem occurred with one of the argument values. Make sure that the arguments used are correct, try to change the value and evaluate the result.

#NIL! You have specified an intersection between ranges that are not in contact. This is a reference problem. If you integrate several cell ranges in a function (e.g.: *SUM (C1:C10, E12:G15)*), make sure you separate the ranges by a comma, as indicated. Otherwise, Excel will try to add the cells shared by the two ranges.

#REF! The cell reference is not valid. Change the formula or cancel the last operation if you have deleted a cell from the formula.

#VALUE You have used an incorrect type of argument or operand.

		Outgoing	
Type	VAT excl	VAT rate	Global VAT
Facture	1,200.00 €	21%	252.00 €
Facture	1,600.00 €	21%	336.00 €
Facture	480.00 €	21%	100.80 €
Facture	625.00 €	21%	131.25 €
Ref.	Total VAT excl		Total VAT
	###########		820.05 €

Tools / Auditing

Tools / Spelling

Excel 2000: Insert / Function

Inserting a conditional function

The underlying principle here is: if the condition is met (a comparison operator is used), the spreadsheet displays *Result A*. If the condition is not met, it displays *Result B*. Let us assume that students must get an average of 11/20 to pass. If the result is less than 11, Excel will display 'You are a disgrace to your school'. If the result is above, it will display the message 'Congratulations, you have passed'.

To insert a conditional function:

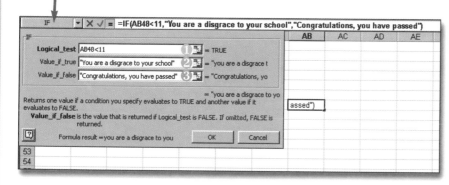

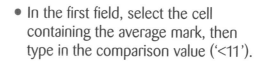

① Formula condition
② Result A
③ Result B

- Run the Insert/Function command, and select IF in the LOGICAL heading.

- In the first field, select the cell containing the average mark, then type in the comparison value ('<11').

- In the second field, enter the sentence to display if the value meets the condition, and in the third field, the text if the value does not meet the condition.

- The formula bar displays the entire condition.

Insert menu:
- Cells...
- Rows
- Columns
- Worksheet
- Chart...
- Page Break
- Function...
- Name
- Comment
- Picture
- Object...
- Hyperlink...   Ctrl+K

Excel allows you to save up to seven conditional functions for combining the alternatives. In such a case, the first argument is a single argument, while the second is replaced by a function (containing two arguments, which raises the total number of alternatives to three).

A1 ▼ =

To access named ranges:

Press the *F5* key or select Edit/Go To. Now just click on one of the referenced tables to indicate your choice, then click OK to select and display it on the screen.

To delete a range name:

Run the Insert/Name/Define command. To delete a reference (which has no influence on the contents of the spreadsheet), select it in the list, then click the Delete button. **Warning:** the deletion is irreversible and Excel does not ask for any confirmation.

To change a range name:

Run the Insert/Name Define command. You can change the name or the reference (and the range of cells linked to the name, etc.). To change the name, click on it in the list to select it and enter the new name. Click Add.

To change a reference without changing name:

- In the same dialogue box, click the minimize button of the Refers to heading to return to the spreadsheet. Select the range to which the name refers.

- When you close the floating toolbar, you return automatically to the initial dialogue box.

- Click OK to confirm the changes.

Edit / Go To:

Insert / Name / Create

Excel 2000: Insert / Name / Define

Name cell ranges

If the spreadsheet is expanded and filled, giving a name to ranges of cells will save you valuable time when working in and structuring the spreadsheet. In this way, you can find any selection (from one cell to several worksheets) from the name you have given; Excel will adjust the display if the zoom value in force is not appropriate. When you enter the name of a range, avoid blank spaces (replaced, as you will have noted, by an underline character '_') and the following characters: *Slash* (/) and *Back-Slash* (\); punctuation marks (? ; and " "), operation signs (*), comparators (> and <) and vertical bar (|). The names of the cell ranges cannot exceed 255 characters.

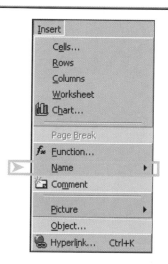

To name a range:

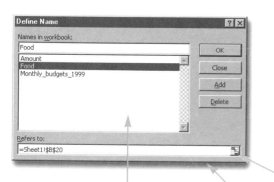

- Select the Insert/Name/Define command.

- Type a precise name in the Names in workbook field.

- Click the minimise button of the Refers to heading to return to the spreadsheet. Select the range to which the name refers.

- Click the Restore button of the floating toolbar to return to the dialogue box.

- Click Add to insert the name in the list.

minimise button

'Names in workbook' field   'Refers to' field

Sheet1 Sheet2 Sheet3

Fractions:

You can convert decimals into fractions if necessary. The precision of the fractions is up to you. Excel will round off the fractions according to the type selected. Whole numbers are accepted, and only numbers behind the decimal point are converted. In a cell, the whole number is aligned left and the fraction right.

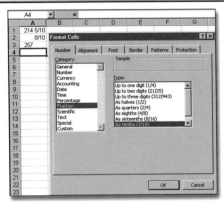

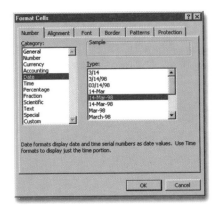

Date and automatic format:

When you enter a date in a cell, you must separate the numbers representing days, months and years by a forward slash '/' or a hyphen '-'. To indicate *14 February 1977*, you must enter the information as follows: *14/02/77* or *14/02/1977* or *14-Feb-1977*.

When the spreadsheet has recognised the encoding of a date, it will automatically change the cell format from General (the default format) to Date. It will also align the information to the right.

Time:

To encode time, you must separate the hours, minutes and seconds by a colon ':' and you can use the Anglo-American notation *AM* and *PM*. For example, to indicate *13 hours 12 minutes and 45 seconds*, enter the information *13:12:45* or *1:12:45 PM*. As soon as the spreadsheet recognises the time, it attributes the Time format to the cell and aligns the information to the right.

Sheet1 / Sheet2 / Sheet3 /

Excel 2000: Format / Cells

Formatting numbers

You can use the Number tab to change the way numbers are displayed and improve the presentation (with or without decimals, with or without the currency symbol, negative numbers displayed in red, etc.). Excel considers by default that all numbers entered in the cell are in General format, i.e. without any specific format. However, Excel does recognise currency, percentage, time, fraction and other formats.

To apply a format (currency, for example):

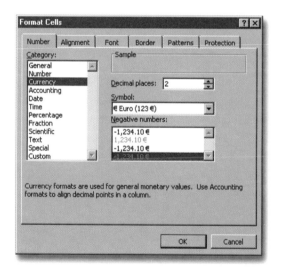

- Select the cell, cell range, row(s) or column(s) before you choose the format.

Format/Cells

- Point at the selection with the cursor and run the Format/Cells command.

- Click the Number tab (it should be displayed by default).

- Select the Currency category. The various currency format options appear on the screen.

- Select the number of decimals to display using the arrows in the Decimal places field.

- Select a currency symbol. This symbol appears before or after the number in each of the selected cells. The search is carried out by country. Note that some formulas allow you to draw up a currency exchange worksheet.

- Select the Negative Numbers display.

- Click OK to confirm your choices and apply them to the selected cells.

Orientation:

The Alignment tab in the dialogue box is used to change the orientation of the text in a cell. This is indispensable if you want articles displayed vertically or at a 45° angle in a cell. To obtain this effect, click on the red diamond and pivot the Text bar while holding down the mouse button.

▷ **To change the orientation of titles:**

- Select the tables of the worksheet.
- Run the Format/Cells command and click the Alignment tab.
- Enter the value *45* in the degrees field or use the red diamond to change the angle of orientation.
- Select the new angle of orientation by clicking OK. Excel will automatically change the height of the rows.

Merging cells:

When you merge cells, you combine several cells into a single one. In this way you can create a title that takes up the entire width of a worksheet. Only the data displayed in the upper left-hand corner (reference cell) are kept.

▷ **To merge cells:**

- Enter the data (e.g. a title) in the upper left-hand cell.
- Select all the cells you want to merge (at least two).
- Run the Format/Cells command, Alignment tab and tick the Merge Cells box.
- Click OK.

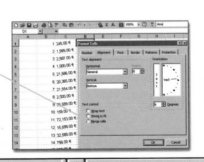

Edit / Delete / Formats

Sheet1 / Sheet2 / Sheet3

Excel 2000: Format / Cells

Formatting cells

By default, Excel displays text in *Arial 10*. Arial is the name of the font, 10 is the font size in typographic points. To highlight characters, you can change their size, font or colour. All the font formatting options are found under the Font tab.

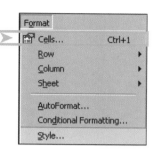

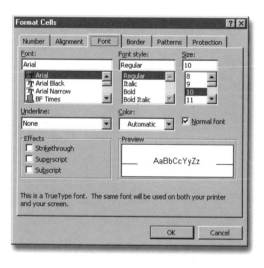

To format fonts:

- Select the cells to edit.

- Select the Format/Cells command and click the Font tab. In the Font header, click on a font to select it.

- Click on a size in the Size drop-down menu to change the font size.

- To display text in italics, select the italics option in the Style menu.

- The formatting is complete.

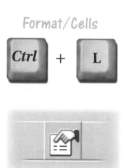

Format/Cells

Ctrl + L

The main formatting attributes are accessible at all times through icons in the toolbar. From left to right, there is a drop-down menu for the fonts, another for the font size, and three icons to put the contents of the selected cells in bold face, italics and underline.

Background colour

Excel allows you to choose a background colour for the cells through a *'colour palette.'* This window, also used to change the colour of fonts and borders, displays all the colours available in Excel.

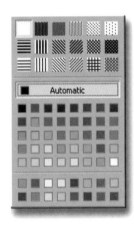

To select the background colour:

- Select the cells to colour.

- Choose Format/Cells and then click the Patterns tab.

- Select the background colour you want by clicking on it in the palette.

- You can choose a pattern colour and a pattern (gridlines, stripes, etc.). Select one that goes together with the background. Bear in mind that if no pattern is selected, only the background appears.

- Click OK to confirm the colour and apply it.

Using colours:

Colours add life to a worksheet displayed on the screen. If, however, you print the spreadsheet with a conventional printer (black and white laser printer), avoid using dark colours (unless you display text in white, for example). Converted to grey levels, these colours tend to turn black, thereby hiding the text and consuming an impressive quantity of ink.

Format / Cells
(Border tab and Font tab)

68

69

| A1 | ▼ | = |

Formatting gridlines

The light gridlines are displayed on the screen solely for the sake of clarity and legibility: they are not printable. When you compose a worksheet, you can colour frames, borders and cells. To access these options, click the Border tab in the Format/Cells dialogue box.

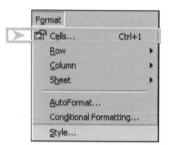

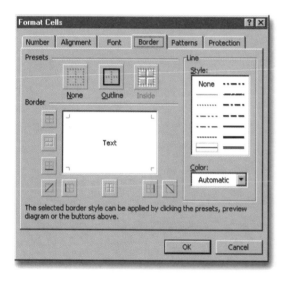

To define gridlines:

- Select the entire worksheet

- Run the Format/Cells command and click the Border tab.

- Prepare your work by choosing a line style in the heading of the same name.

- Continue by selecting a border colour in the Color drop-down menu, which displays a colour palette (see next page). The line styles change colour.

- Indicate to Excel the borders to draw. If you opt for a simple frame around the worksheet, click Outline under the Presets heading. Change the line style and colour before you select the Inside option in the Presets heading. In Excel you can customise the borders by clicking directly in the preview area.

- Click OK to confirm the changes.

Format/Cells

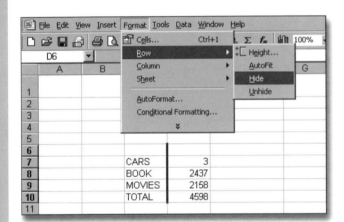

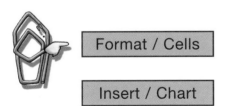

Format / Cells

Insert / Chart

AutoFit:

To automatically fit the width of a column in the cell that contains the most data, run the Format/Column/AutoFit Selection command.

To hide a column or a row:

Excel suggests that you improve the presentation of the worksheet by temporarily hiding rows or columns of secondary importance. This can prove useful when you insert a chart, because you keep only the main data (the '*trends*'). If you prepare a worksheet in advance by hiding superfluous information, you will produce clear, pertinent charts. To hide a row temporarily, select it (just place the selector in one of the row cells) and use the Format/ Row/Hide command. The hidden items are not deleted. You can make them reappear easily with the Format/Row/Unhide command.

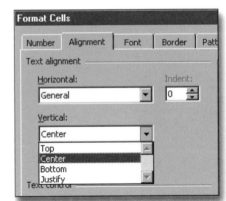

Vertical alignment of the content:

The vertical alignment of the content of the cells does not fall under row formatting. The appropriate options are contained in the Alignment tab of the Format/Cells dialogue box. Select the alignment in the Text alignment/Vertical drop-down menu.

Excel 2000: Format / Row (columm)

Formatting rows (columns)

Everything introduced in these pages applies equally to rows and columns. You can ask Excel to adjust the width of columns or the height of rows so as to make all the characters or numbers in the cells more visible.

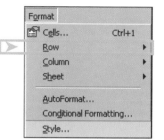

To change the height of a row:

- Select the row and run the Format/Row/Height command (to change the column width: select Format/Column/Width).

- Specify the height in points (a typographic unit; the font size is expressed in points) for the selected rows.

- Click OK to confirm the new height.

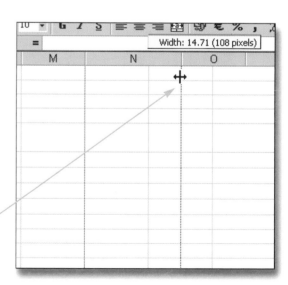

You can also proceed manually with the mouse. Place the pointer on the line separating two columns or two rows. The pointer turns into a black arrowed bar. Click and drag the mouse: the separation bar follows the movement (dotted lines indicate the width of the column if you were to release the mouse button). A bubble displays the value of the new width. You actually change the width of the column to the left of the bar, as the columns to the right are not narrowed down but simply pushed back.

> *The cursor is placed on the line separating the columns 'N' and 'O'. Move it to the left to widen Column 'O' or to the right to widen Column 'N'.*

Styles

A style automatically formats the characters as if you had gone through all the tabs in the Format/Cells dialogue box. By attributing a style to one or more cells, you apply a consistent format according to the type of data contained.

To apply a style:

- Select the cells on which to apply the style.
- Run Format/Style.
- In the drop-down menu, select the style you want to apply.
- All the check boxes contain preset attributes. Only the ticked attributes are active. Tick or untick the check boxes according to your needs.
- Click OK to apply the style to the selection.

Type of data

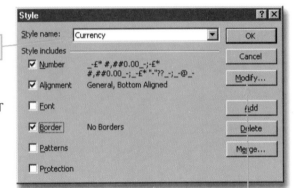

Modify button

To create (or modify) a style:

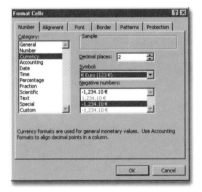

- Click in the Style name heading (above the drop-down menu) and enter the name of the new style.
- By default, Excel always attributes the characteristics of the previously selected style.
- Click the Modify button to display the Format/Cells dialogue box and modify all the desired settings.
- Click OK to return to the style dialogue box.
- Click Add to confirm the changes.
- Click OK to create the style and apply it to the selection.

Format / Cells

72

Excel 2000: Format / Autofit

Autoformatting a worksheet

Excel contains a complete worksheet formatting catalogue, depending on the nature or function of the sheets. You can format borders, background, indents, font, font style and font size, cell width and height, etc. at a click of the mouse. And you can always change one attribute or another manually.

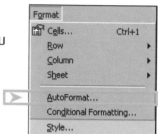

To format a worksheet:

- Select all the cells in the worksheet.

- Run Format/Autoformat.

- Click the format you want.

- If you think that the worksheet of your choice is too elaborate, get rid of the attributes you don't like. A heading entitled Formats to apply contains several boxes already ticked. To access it, click the Options button. Untick the check box(es) corresponding to the attribute(s) you want to get rid of.

- The preview box of each worksheet displays the changes immediately.

- Click OK to confirm the format.

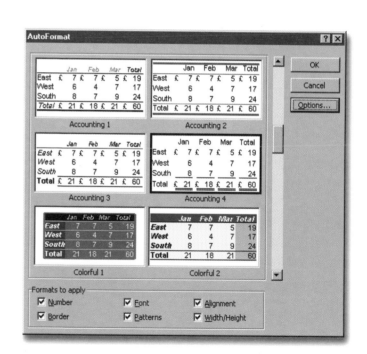

Multiple conditions:

In the Conditional Formatting dialogue box you can define up to three conditions simultaneously. In this way, only items that meet the two or three conditions will adopt the formatting. To add conditions, click the Add button and enter the conditions as explained above. Avoid contradictory conditions!

To delete a condition, click the Delete button; a tiny dialogue box with a list of conditions will open, asking you to select the conditions you want to delete.

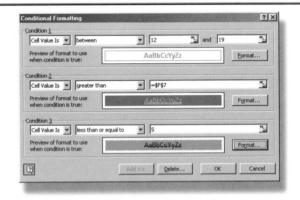

Example:

Let us suppose that a couple want to enter in Excel the pocket money they give their children. All they have to do is fix a top limit, e.g. £5.00, above which the source will dry up automatically, and ask Excel to display in red those cells whose content exceeds £5.00. In this case, the condition set will be: 'Cell Value Is greater than or equal to.' When they have entered more than £5.00, the characters will appear in red. In the meantime, they retain their current attributes.

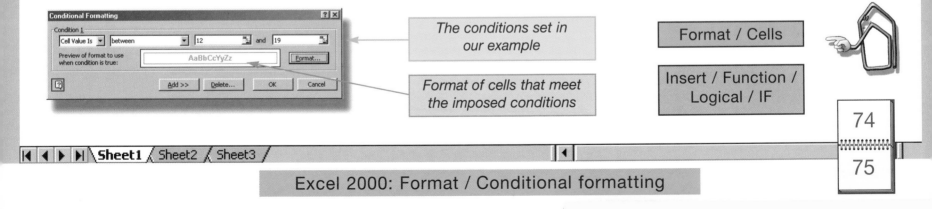

The conditions set in our example

Format of cells that meet the imposed conditions

Format / Cells

Insert / Function / Logical / IF

74

75

| A1 | ▼ | = | |

Conditional formatting

Conditional formatting is a complete formatting (borders, characters, etc.) which is only applied to a cell whose contents meet a condition you have specified.

To prepare a conditional formatting :

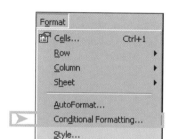

- Select the cells for the condition you will set.

- Select the Format/Conditional Formatting command.

- Select the contents to compare: the value of the cell or the formula (in which case, the result can only be *TRUE* or *FALSE*).

- Select a comparator: *Is equal to*, *Is less than*, etc.

- Enter the comparison value or click on the minimize icon and select a cell in the worksheet. The contents of this cell will serve as the point of comparison, even if it changes.

- Click the Format button to open a dialogue box similar to Format/Cells, from which you can access the options of the Font, Border and Pattern tabs.

- Select the formatting options of your choice and click OK to confirm the attributes.

- The Format Preview displays a preview of the selected formatting attributes.

- Click OK to confirm.

Formatting a spreadsheet

The spreadsheet formatting possibilities are limited. However, with Excel, you can insert wallpaper to liven up your spreadsheet. One small inconvenience, though, is that wallpaper rarely makes data easier to read.

- Click the spreadsheet tab. Note that Excel will apply the wallpaper only to the selected sheet. You can thus use various wallpapers in the same workbook.

- Use the Format/Sheet/Background command.

- Excel opens an exploring window, which, you will remember, enables you to browse in the hard disk and locate a file.

- Use the icons to locate an image file. Excel accepts the main types of images (JPEG, BMP, GIF, TIFF, EPS, CorelDRAW, etc.).

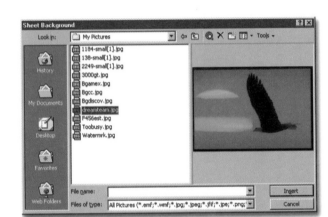

- Click Open to display the image in the background.

- Excel establishes the image directly.

- Use a fill colour for cells that contain data, as illustrated in the image opposite. In this case, we have used white for clarity.

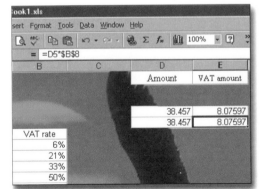

To delete a background:

To get rid of a background, click the Format/Sheet/Delete Background command.

Excel 2000: Format / Sheet / Hide

Sheet1 / Sheet2 / Sheet3

Formatting spreadsheets

Excel can temporarily hide spreadsheets in a workbook. You thus avoid overloading the workbook with sheets that entail intermediate operations or contain temporary information. When the sheet is hidden, its tab disappears from the screen. Naturally, the information stored on the sheet is not lost; it is simply not displayed.

To hide a sheet:

- Click the tab of the sheet you want to hide.

- Run the Format/Sheet/Hide command. Excel hides the sheet and its tab from the screen.

To unhide the sheet:

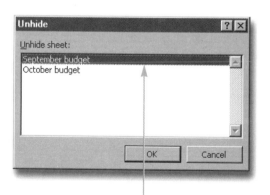

- Use the Format/Sheet/Unhide command to redisplay the View dialogue box.

- In the list displayed by the box, click the sheet to view in the workbook.

- Click OK to confirm the operation. Excel will redisplay the sheet in the workbook.

You can hide several sheets in a single operation. Just select them by keeping *Ctrl* pressed and clicking each of the tabs. The Format/Sheet/Hide command hides all the selected sheets. The same logic also applies to unhiding sheets.

Select the sheet
to unhide

Foreign languages:

Excel 2000 contains an English spell-checking dictionary. If you have the *Office 2000 MultiLanguage Pack*, then your program can correct many foreign languages. To change a language use the Tools/Spelling command. In the Dictionary Language drop-down menu, click the language of your choice. Now click Close and restart the spell checking.

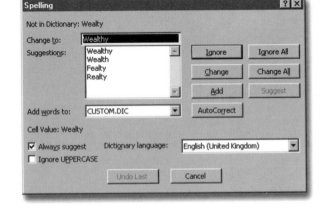

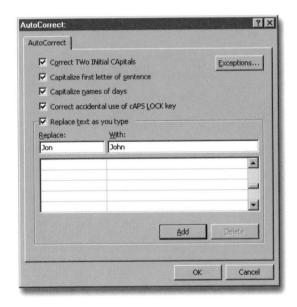

AutoCorrect:

The Tools/AutoCorrect command contains a list of common errors and typos. As you type, Excel will correct any misspelled words it contains automatically.

- Use the Tools/AutoCorrect command.
- In the Replace field, enter the incorrect word.
- In the By field, enter the correct word.
- Click Add to insert the word and its correction in the AutoCorrect list.
- Tick Replace text as you type.
- Click OK to confirm the changes and exit the window.

Tools / AutoCorrect

A1 ▼ =

Checking spelling in the cells

During the spell-check, Excel 2000 consults its internal dictionary. It may fail to find specialised words, proper names, etc., but is efficient for the usual vocabulary. The words it does not recognise are displayed in the checking window. You must tell Excel to correct, keep or add a word to its dictionary.

To check the spelling of cell contents:

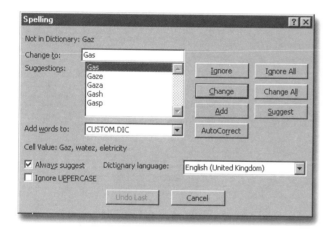

- Select the Tools/Spelling command.

- Excel displays the first word not contained in its dictionary. A list of similar words is displayed in the Suggestions area.

- To correct this word, choose one of the Excel suggestions. If none is given, select the misspelled word in the Change to window and change it manually.

- Click Change. Excel displays the next misspelled word. To change all the occurrences of the unknown word in the spreadsheet, click Change All.

- To avoid changing a word that is correct, but not known to Excel, click Ignore (or Ignore All to pass over all these occurrences).

- Click Close to finish.

Tools / Spelling

Note

When you click Add, you enter the word considered incorrect into the Excel dictionary.

Conversion into Euros

Excel 2000 provides an automatic converter of the main European currencies into euros.

To convert a value from pounds into euros:

- Select the host cell of the converted currency.
- Select the Tools/Euro Conversion command to open the dialogue box to the right:

- Place the mouse pointer in the Source range, click the minimise button and select the cell containing the amount in pounds. The absolute address of this cell appears in the text field.
- Place the mouse pointer in the Destination range and click in the host cell of the amount in Euros.
- The absolute address of this cell appears in the text field.
- In the From heading, select pounds if the value is denominated in **GBP**.
- In the To heading, select the euro from the drop-down menu.
- Select an Output Format if you want to modify the default setting in Excel.
- Click OK.

Insert / Function

Excel 2000: Tools / Goal Seek

A1 =

Defining Goal Seek

Excel can be used to set a target (goal seek) and to calculate the value of an unknown item in its formula. Imagine two brothers who have to reimburse £10,000.00 to a bookmaker. The first can pay £50.00 a month, the second £62.50. How many months will it take for them to pay back their debt? Excel provides the answer instantly. You must create the formula calculating the total reimbursement of £10,000.00 [$(50+62.50)*x=10,000$], and make sure you do not get mixed up when selecting the cells that contain the data!

To calculate a component:

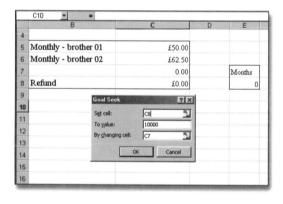

- Prepare the formula and place the data in the referenced cells (or work directly with fixed values typed in).

- Click the cell you want to define.

- Now enter the goal seek (*target value: £10,000.00*).

- Finally, select the cell that contains the data to calculate.

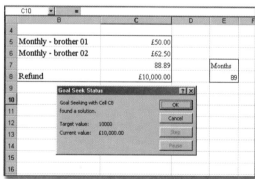

- Click OK.

- Excel displays a window indicating that it has found a result.

- We have used the mathematical function ROUNDUP to automatically round up the month number to the higher unit.

Tracing an error

5	Monthly - brother 01	50.00 €
6	Monthly - brother 02	62.50 €
7		
8	Refund	0.00 €
9		
10	Already paid	225.30 €
11		
12	Advance no 1	0.30 €
13		
14	Advance / Refund ratio	#DIV/0!
15		
16	Credit on account	#DIV/0!

The trace error feature traces the source of the error. Select a cell containing an error and run the Tools/ Auditing/Trace error command. Here once again, the blue and red arrows specify the point from which the error is obtained. You will usually have to change the precedents of this cell to put things right.
You can also display the dependents of a cell so that you can view its impact on calculations downstream.

To remove arrows:

To remove all arrows, use the Tools/Auditing/Remove all arrows command. If you want to remove only the arrows to the precedents of the selected cells, click the Remove precedent arrows (in the Auditing toolbar).

Toolbar:

To have all the commands you need for the auditing, simply activate the Tools/Auditing/Show Auditing Toolbar.

What to do:

When you have traced the error that causes the failure of all the dependent formulas, correct it manually.

Tools / Auditing / Show Auditing Toolbar

Excel 2000: Tools / Auditing

Sheet1 / Sheet2 / Sheet3 /

| A1 | ▼ | = | |

Checking the formulas

A cell does not normally display the result of a formula with two fixed values entered manually. It integrates the result in other formulas and its own result will be used by other cells. The auditing feature traces dependent formulas (dependents), precedent formulas (precedents) or any errors starting from a selected cell. It essentially retraces the history of an incorrect result you have selected and its repercussions. To enable you to view the source of the problem, Excel links the cells involved using blue and black arrows if the formula refers to a value in another spreadsheet.

C10	▼	=	=((C5+C6)*E8)+C12	
	B	C	D	E
4				
5	Monthly - brother 01	50.00 €		
6	Monthly - brother 02	62.50 €		
7				Months
8	Refund	0.00 €		2
9				
10	Already paid	225.30 €		
11				
12	Advance no 1	0.30 €		
13				
14	Advance / Refund ratio			

To trace precedents:

- Select a cell.

- Use the Tools/Auditing/Trace precedents command to view the values or results that have produced the result displayed.

- Excel uses arrows to indicate the cells involved in the calculation of the result. Note that, with this command, you can only go back to the direct precedent. To display the precedents of precedents, you must select a precedent cell and use this command again.

Deleting a list / Adding to a list

To delete a list, select it under Custom Lists and click the Delete button. If you delete a list by mistake, close the dialogue box and click Undo to retrieve it.

To add items:

To add a word to a list, place the insertion point (blinking vertical bar) anywhere in the list, press Enter to go to the row (thereby creating a new blank row ready to receive characters) and complete the list. Click Add, and then click OK. In the same way, you can delete items or correct spelling errors, for example.

Warning: Enter your changes and then click Add (not Delete, because you would delete the entire list!).

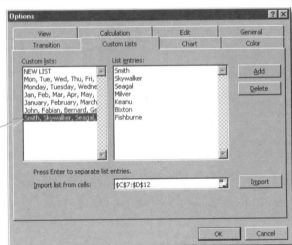

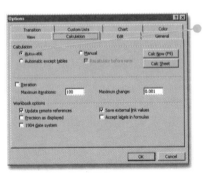

To carry out calculations:

Excel automatically calculates (by default) the results of all the formulas it contains. If it does not, you can ask it to calculate a formula immediately by pressing the F9 key. To start the calculation, open the Tools/Options dialogue box and select the calculation tab. Tick the Automatic option under the Calculation heading.

Insert / Name / Define

84

85

Excel 2000: Tools / Options / Custom Lists

Creating custom lists

If the lists in Excel are not enough, you can always create your own list. A grocer, for example, could create an automatic list per section to make it easier for him to prepare each inventory or command.

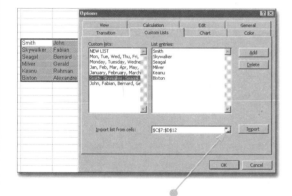

To create a custom list:

- Enter all the names of articles (or members, etc.) in a blank sheet of a workbook. You need only carry out this operation once. Select the list.

- Run the Tools/Options command to display the Options dialogue box.

- Click the Custom Lists tab.

- The Import list from cells field displays the (absolute) references of the selected cells. Select the list by clicking the minimise button of the field (on the right).

- Click the Import button to confirm the new list.

- Click OK to close the Options dialogue box; the list is placed in the Custom list heading and can now be used.

- The next time you want to enter the list of names in a workbook, all you have to do is enter the first name and use the fill handle (black cross, lower right corner of the cell) and the spreadsheet will automatically enter the other names.

Encoding data

In its real form, a database is structured as a worksheet, the first row of which contains the fields (or titles of columns, if you prefer). These fields indicate the nature of the contents of the column cells. You can use sheets rather than tables if you prefer. Each sheet presents the data contained in the cells of a record (a row) in a different way.

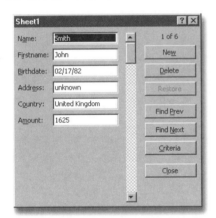

Sheet

To view the contents of a worksheet, activate Data/Form (make sure that you select the entire worksheet and do not forget the title row).

To create a new sheet:

Name	Firstname	Birthdate	Address	Country	Amount
Smith	John	02/17/82	unknown	United Kingdom	1,625.00 €
Skywalker	Fabian	05/01/82	unknown	United Kingdom	2,865.00 €
Seagal	Bernard	01/04/73	unknown	United Kingdom	3,564.00 €
Milver	Gerald	08/16/74	unknown	United Kingdom	1,258.00 €
Keanu	Rahman	06/21/81	unknown	United Kingdom	5,689.00 €

Form

- Select the worksheet.

- Activate the Data/Form command.

- Click New.

- Fill the text fields (Excel displays the categories). Click Close.

- Excel returns to the table and displays an additional row at the bottom of the worksheet.

To delete a form:

- Point the mouse at the form you want to delete and click Delete.

- Excel displays a message saying 'the record will be definitively deleted'. If this is what you want, click Yes. Otherwise, click No.

Data / Form

Data / Filter

Excel 2000: Data / Sort

Sorting data

Excel is also used as a small database. It therefore contains specific tools such as row sorting (using a column you indicate as a reference) in ascending or descending order, according to your choice. Excel recognises and sorts alphanumeric (text and date) and numeric data.

To sort the data of a worksheet:

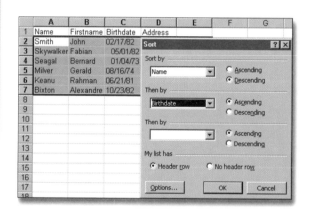

- Select the part of the worksheet to sort. Do not select just one column. In such a case, only the data of that column will be sorted; the rows will no longer correspond.

- Run the Data/Form command.

- The first row of a worksheet often contains column titles. If this title row is part of the selection, click Yes. If not, click No in the Title Row heading.

- Select the reference column for the sorting operation (1st key drop-down menu). If you have not included the title row in the selection, the drop-down menu will indicate Column 1, Column 2, etc.

- Choose the type of sorting order: ascending or descending.

- If necessary, start the procedure all over again to define the settings of a second sorting key.

- Click OK to launch the sorting operation.

To view the entire worksheet:

To return to the entire worksheet, select the option (All) in the drop-down menu with the blue arrow (this arrow indicates that it served as reference for the last filtering operation).

To make the arrows that indicate the presence of drop-down menus disappear, tick the Data/Filter/AutoFilter command (which is preceded by a ✓).

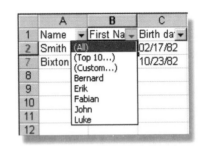

To filter according to a conditional criterion:

You can filter records on the basis of a condition you define using the trio: 'If...' 'comparison operator' 'value.'

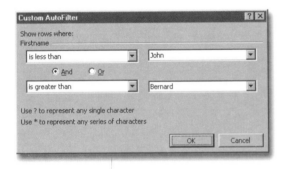

To set a conditional filter:

- Activate the Data/Filter/AutoFilter command.
- In the drop-down menu, activate the Customized command. It opens a condition dialogue box.
- The first heading of this dialogue box takes the name of the column whose menu you have dropped down.
- In the drop-down menu, select a comparator (greater than, equal to, etc.) which will filter the items by numerical or alphabetical order.

- In the second drop-down menu, type in the value or choose one from the menu.
- If necessary, select a link agent and then set a second condition.
- Click OK to confirm this filter and apply it to the column.

Data / Sort

88

Filtering data

By filtering records, you can display only those items that meet a condition. In this way, only pertinent data is displayed. Records that have not met the filter's requirements are not deleted, but simply hidden by Excel.

To keep records that display a specified value:

- Select the worksheet that contains the items to filter.

- Run Data/Filter/AutoFilter command. All the cells of the title row are given a down arrow. This drop-down menu displays various values in the column, arranged in order. They will serve as a reference to Excel to filter the records.

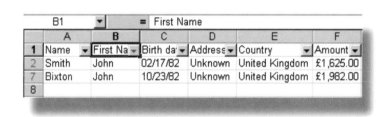

- Drop down the menu of a column.

- Click the value you want.

- Excel hides all the records whose contents (in the appropriate column) do not correspond to the selected value. Note that Excel keeps the row number of the records, and displays it in blue in the row header (left edge of the screen).

- When a sorting criterion is selected, the drop-down menus of the other column headers keep only the values displayed by the records that have passed the filtering test.

Help

When you click on any of the options of the Office Assistant, you will open a help window containing three tabs: Contents, Answer Wizard and Index.

- The Contents tab contains all the topics listed by subject (Internet, Format, etc.) in booklets. Click on the booklet to view all the topics, then click on a topic to have it displayed in a window.

- In the Answer Wizard tab, you can widen your knowledge of Excel by viewing, one by one, all the topics dealing with your query.

- To find a given word, you must use the Index, which contains a list of all the words contained in Help. Excel limits the scope of the search and shows the words corresponding to the characters already entered. Simply click on a keyword and then on a topic. Finally, click the Search button to view the topic you have selected.

Context-sensitive help

This feature is used in most dialogue boxes, where it appears as a question mark. When you click on this icon ('?'), the mouse pointer turns into an arrowed question mark. Ask Excel 2000 about an unknown item or one that requires some additional information by clicking it with this new cursor. A pop-up box appears with the relevant information – very useful to find out what all the various functions and menus actually do.

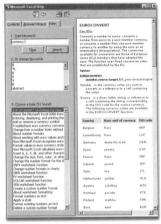

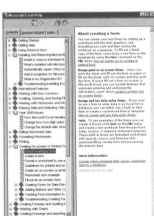

Index, left, and Answer Wizard, below right.

Contents, left.

Getting help

Excel 2000 will almost never let you down, because it offers all types of help. However, the sheer volume of information in the different help windows is such that you can easily get lost. So before you start looking for help, bear in mind these two basic rules:

⇨ Never lose sight of your objective, because, if you do, you are likely to get lost as you proceed from link to link.

⇨ Use the right help tool for the information you want.
- If you only want a word of explanation on a topic in the dialogue box, then use the context-sensitive help.
- If you want to review a complicated procedure, use the Index to go directly to that procedure.
- If you want to collect all the information on statistical functions, use the Search function, which will draw up a list of all the related pages for you.

The Office Assistant

When you press F1, the Office Assistant (a character called Clippit) appears.
His role is to help you when you run into problems.

Search

When you need help, left-click Clippit and ask him a simple question using Excel vocabulary if possible (e.g. click, formula not calculation, border not frame, etc.). Now click the Search button. Depending on the topic, the precision of your question and the answers it has in store, Clippit will suggest one or more topics.

For more information on a given point, click the blue button next to the desired data.

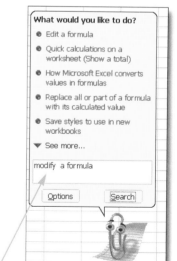

Excel 2000: Index

94
95

Excel 2000: Index

INDEX - INDEX - INDEX - INDEX - INDEX - INDEX - INDEX - INDEX - INDEX

SHORTCUT KEYS

MOVING THE INSERTION POINT IN A SPREADSHEET

In the first cell of a row	Home
In the cell A1	Ctrl+Home
Go to a cell whose address you know	F5

SELECT

Active row	Shift+Space
Active column	Ctrl+Space
Extend selection to neighbouring cell	Shift+Arrow

CANCEL

Cancel last action	Ctrl+Z

CELL CONTENTS

Edit a cell	F2
Hard return in a cell	Alt+Enter
Cancel changes	Esc
Enter the day's date (fixed)	Ctrl+;

CLIPBOARD

Copy	Ctrl+C
Cut	Ctrl+X
Paste	Ctrl+V

FORMATS

Boldface	Ctrl+G
Italics	Ctrl+I
Underline	Ctrl+U
Percentage	Ctrl+%
Thousand and decimal separator	Ctrl+!
Frame range of selected cells	Ctrl+0

PRINT AND SAVE

Print	Ctrl+P
Create new workbook	Ctrl+N
Open a workbook	Ctrl+O
Save a workbook	Ctrl+S

Sheet1 / Sheet2 / Sheet3 /

Excel 2000: Shortcut keys